YORKSHIRE:
THE WEST RIDING

YORKSHIRE:
THE WEST RIDING

DAVID H. PILL

B. T. Batsford Ltd
London

To past and present colleagues and students
at Greenhead High School and Greenhead College, Huddersfield.

First published 1977
© David H. Pill 1977
Printed in Great Britain by The Pitman Press Ltd., Bath
for the publishers B. T. Batsford Ltd
4 Fitzhardinge Street, London W1H 0AH

ISBN 0 7134 3188 1

CONTENTS

	Map of the West Riding	6
	List of Illustrations	8
	Acknowledgements	9
	Introduction	11
One	The Plain – Selby and Boothferry	28
Two	The Dales – Harrogate and Craven	49
Three	West of the Pennines – Sedbergh, Bowland and Saddleworth	74
Four	Kirklees	91
Five	Calderdale	106
Six	Bradford	121
Seven	Leeds	131
Eight	Wakefield	153
Nine	Barnsley	166
Ten	Sheffield	176
Eleven	Rotherham	184
Twelve	Doncaster	193
	Index	201

WEST RIDING

ILLUSTRATIONS

1	Cray, upper Wharfedale	17
2	Norman doorway, Adel church	18
3	West door, Selby Abbey	18
4	Cloisters, Kirkstall Abbey	18
5	Ripon Cathedral	35
6	Fountains Abbey	35
7	Brimham Rocks	36
8	Knaresborough	53
9	The River Wharfe at Bolton Abbey	54
10	Heptonstall datestone	71
11	Font carving, Aston church	71
12	Monument detail, Great Mitton church	71
13	Cartwright Hall, Bradford	72
14	The Piece Hall, Halifax	72
15	Skipton Castle	72
16	Temple Newsam	89
17	Bishopthorpe Palace	89
18	Bramham Park	90
19	Harewood House	90
20	Leeds Town Hall	107
21	Wakefield Cathedral	108
22	Sheffield Cathedral	141
23	Tickhill church	142
24	Dent Town	159
25	Pontefract market place	159
26	Stoodley Pike, upper Calderdale	159
27	Boroughbridge	160
28	Moors above Haworth	160

ACKNOWLEDGEMENTS

It is a pleasure to be able to acknowledge the help I have had from many people in the writing of this book. All my enquiries have met with a kindly reception, and I am particularly grateful to the staff of Kirklees Central Library and to the Rev. Edward Simpson for letting me draw on his own extensive collection of books on the West Riding, and also to the officers of the Boothferry, Craven and Selby District Councils and of the County Councils of North and South Yorkshire, and in the latter case particularly to the Chief Executive, Mr F. A. Mallett, and to Mr Gilmour and Mr Munford of the Department of Recreation, Culture and Health. I am also grateful to the staff of John Smith's and Sam Smith's breweries, and especially to Mrs Margaret Hields of John Smith's, who went to a great deal of trouble to help me. I have met some very kind and friendly people on my journeys, like Mr Richard Moody, who took me on a conducted tour of Selby (and missed a dental appointment in doing so), and Mr D. C. Eyre, who provided me with information about the recent excavations in the town. A number of clergy and ministers have also gone out of their way to help me, particularly the clergy of Christ Church, Harrogate and St Giles', Pontefract, and Rabbi Heilbron of Bradford Synagogue. Thanks are also due to my former colleague Miss K.M. Cocker for information on certain historical matters, and to those other friends who have kindly and patiently ferried a non-motorist about the Riding, Mr David Newton, Mr Val Roche, Mr Peter Simpson, and Mr Michael Rayner, who also very kindly agreed to read the proofs. I have relied on the guidance of a large number of books in the writing of this one and I feel bound to acknowledge my particular debt to the work of Sir Nikolaus Pevsner and Dr Arthur Raistrick. Finally, an apology to those readers whose interesting villages and towns I have not mentioned in the text. Todwick, Bradfield, Thorpe Salvin, Darrington and Womersley immediately come to mind. Perhaps I will have the opportunity to do them justice on some other occasion.

The author and publishers would also like to thank the following for permission to reproduce the pictures in the book: J. Allan Cash Ltd, no. 5; Peter Baker, no. 8; A. F. Kersting, nos. 6, 9, 11, 12, 18, 22; Clifford Robinson, nos. 2, 7, 10, 13, 14, 15, 17, 25, 26, 27, 28; Kenneth Scowen, no. 24; Olive Smith, nos. 21, 23; Spectrum, nos. 1, 3, 4, 16, 19, 20.

INTRODUCTION

For eleven hundred years there was a county of York; its boundaries were drawn up by Danish invaders in the 9th century. Danish Yorkshire was an independent kingdom with its own parliament called the *Thing*, held in York city, to which representatives came from each of its three divisions – the North, East and West Ridings. Now the ancient kingdom and largest English county is no more. The Local Government Act, which was passed in an attempt to streamline local administration in 1972 and implemented on 1 April 1974, destroyed what the Danes had created so long ago. No longer are there three ridings, for centuries regarded as counties in their own right. There is a North Yorkshire and a West Yorkshire, but no East Yorkshire. And West Yorkshire is a mere shadow of the old West Riding, whose 2,777 square miles are the subject of this book. The boundary commissioners have divided the Riding up with more logic than they have used in reorganization elsewhere in Britain, but with little regard for local patriotism. The Pennines, that great chain of limestone and gritstone hills often called the backbone of England, have been considered a natural boundary, and three areas of the West Riding lying to the west of them are no longer Yorkshire. The area around Sedbergh in the north-west corner of the county is now in the new county of Cumbria, the royal forest of Bowland has passed into Lancashire, and, despite the local gardeners' protest crop of white roses, Saddleworth Urban District is in the Metropolitan County of Greater Manchester. The largely rural area of the southern Dales and that part of the Vale of York drained by

11

the river Ouse are, with most of the North Riding, in North Yorkshire, while a small portion of the former marshland around the port of Goole is in Humberside, along with most of the old East Riding. The textile belt is a metropolitan county, West Yorkshire, with five administrative districts, Bradford, Calderdale, Kirklees, Leeds and Wakefield, and the coal and steel area to the south is another metropolitan county, South Yorkshire, with four such districts, Barnsley, Doncaster, Rotherham and Sheffield.

The old Yorkshire may have passed away but the Yorkshire spirit has not. Whatever county they now find themselves in, those born in the West Riding still regard themselves as Yorkshiremen. Some of them have helped to found the Ridings Society, refuse to use the new postal addresses, and regularly write letters taking to task for using them the editor of their daily paper, the *Yorkshire Post,* which started as the *Leeds Intelligencer* in 1754 and whose long survival is itself a manifestation of Yorkshire independence. They can at least rejoice that they and their sons remain eligible for that greatest of local honours, playing membership of the Yorkshire County Cricket Club, something to which those born outside the boundaries of the old Yorkshire cannot aspire. The 'tyke' is a rare breed. His superiority goes without saying (although he does have a grudging respect for his almost equally independently minded and hard-working neighbour, the Lancastrian). But like all the English he is a mongrel (though some thoroughbreds may remain in remoter parts). His origins are reflected in the placenames of his county. River names like Ure, Wharfe, Aire, Calder, Colne, Don and Went are British in origin, as are the names of hills like the Chevin and Pen-y-ghent, and were probably in use in one form or another before the Romans set up their legionary fortress at *Eboracum,* now the city of York. *Eboracum* and York may both be forms of the British name *Eburos* – place of the yew tree. When the Romans came, Yorkshire was part of the kingdom of the Brigantes and may have been ruled from Castle Hill in what is now Kirklees, a hill fort which later settlers named Almondbury, meaning perhaps the fort of the old men, i.e. the Britons. For two centuries after the

Romans left, most of the West Riding was in the British kingdom of Elmet, and the names of two villages, Barwick and Sherburn, still have the suffix 'in Elmet'.

It was some time in the 7th century that Elmet was absorbed into another kingdom, Northumbria. This was ruled over by invaders from across the North Sea – the Angles. Their placenames are recognizable from endings such as *ton,* meaning farm, *ley,* meaning clearing, and *bury,* a fortress. Dalton was the farm in the dale, Netherton, the lower farm, Barnsley, Beorn's clearing, and Dewsbury, Dewi's fortified place. Dewi, by the way, was a British personal name, and this and other placenames seem to indicate that some Britons stayed in the area even after the Anglian invasion. The Angles called the Britons the Welsh, or foreigners, and so we have villages called Wales and Walton, both names indicating British occupation, as also does Bretton.

In the 9th century, Danish invaders set up their settlements or *bys* throughout their kingdom of York. Denby means simply Danes' farm. Subsidiary settlements founded by inhabitants of the *bys* were *thorpes,* for example, Skelmanthorpe, Ravensthorpe and Alverthorpe. More Scandinavians arrived from the west in the 10th and 11th centuries. These were Norsemen who had previously settled in Ireland and the Isle of Man and along the Lancashire coast. They made their *thwaites* or clearings on the rough moorsides or in the thick woods that filled the Pennine valleys. Yockenthwaite, Eogan's clearing, shows a clear Norse-Irish link. And the West Riding was not divided into hundreds like other English counties, but into wapentakes, administrative districts created by the Vikings.

The Yorkshireman's brand of English contains many words of Scandinavian origin, and it is this element which helps to make the Yorkshire dialect so distinctive. In the West Riding, streams are *becks,* and narrow valleys are *cloughs* or *gills.* Cowsheds are *mistals* (though this word is probably Norman-French rather than Anglo-Norse in origin), and children at play are said to be *laiking.* The Yorkshireman, no matter what his class, regards his own tongue as standard English and thinks it strange if Bristol Rovers or Chelsea fans look bewildered when asked what colours their team *laike* in. To him a stool is a *buffet,* when he is busy he is *throng,* and when he catches a cold he has been *smittled.* While he is at work, *addling his brass* (earning his money), his wife may be *kaling* (gossiping with other housewives). When her child complains about his food, he is *chuntering,* and when he sulks, he is being *maungy.* Footpaths between fields and buildings are *snickets* and town alleyways are *ginnels.* Streets in the older towns are sometimes called *gates,* not because places like Leeds and Huddersfield ever had town walls, but simply because *gate* is a version of an old Scandinavian word for street. The parish church may be in Kirkgate. (The names of several West Riding villages with ancient churches start with *kirk.*) Several places – Woolley, Selby and Sedbergh are a few – have a Finkle, Finkel or Finkil Street. The name is said to be derived from the Danish for elbow, but since some of these streets have no bend in them, the source of the name may not be the same in every case. 'Fennel hill' has been suggested as an alternative derivation. Experts at Leeds University have made a close study of dialect, even producing a dialect atlas, and they will tell you that it varies slightly from village to village, and when a Bradford or Colne Valley man tells him to go to *Ummer,* perhaps not every native of the West Riding will understand (except maybe from his intonation) that he means him to go to Hell. The inhabitants of the West Riding textile valleys speak with a broader *a* than is usual in most parts of the North and Midlands. Master is m*a*rster an̈d not m*a*ster as in Lancashire, m*ai*ster, as it might be in the Leeds area, or m*e*ster as in Sheffield; plaster is pl*a*rster, and spa is pronounced *spaw.* There is a tendency to pronounce each syllable, so that *nowt,* meaning nothing, pronounced *now-t* in Lancashire, is pronounced *no-ut* in parts of the West Riding. But, as in other parts of England, placenames can cause difficulties for the stranger through abbreviation. Barnoldswick is pronounced *Barlick,* Malham is *Mawm,* Sawley is *Salley,* Golcar is *Goca,* Browsholme is *Brewsome,* Slaithwaite is *Slawit* to a native and *Slathwaite* to anyone else, and Rathmell is *Ramell.*

Actually to be fair to Rathmell we should call it Rathmell-in-England. A legendary farmer, Tommy Johnson, went to sleep on a haystack, it rained, the river Ribble overflowed its banks, and the haystack was carried downstream. Another farmer spotted Tommy and pulled him in. The sleeper awoke to find himself beside what appeared to be a broad lake and did not know where he was. When asked his name, he said 'Tommy Johnson'. 'What, Tommy Johnson o' Ramell?' asked his rescuer. 'Aye, Ramell in England,' he replied. A similar story is told of Wansford-in-England, in Cambridgeshire. Indeed it is strange how often tales, particularly those poking fun at a village, re-occur even within one county. In Huddersfield Junior Library is a series of murals depicting stories told about the foolish behaviour of the people of the Colne Valley. They include the Slaithwaite moonrakers, who thought the moon's reflection was a cheese and tried to rake it out of the canal, and the Marsden 'cuckoos' who tried to build a wall round a cuckoo to prevent it flying away, in the hope of having a perpetual spring. The same story is told of Austwick in Craven. It is also said that when an Austwick farmer's bull got stuck in a gate he sawed its head off to get it out, a tale also told about the Greater Manchester township of Westhoughton. And of several places, including Brighouse, it has been said that the band, on returning from winning a contest late at night, decided to march through the town playing a celebratory tune but took their shoes off so that they would not wake their sleeping neighbours.

Now these legends are being learned by new Yorkshiremen without a drop of Scandinavian blood in their veins. In the last hundred years immigrants have come to the West Riding from all over the world – Polish and Russian Jews fleeing from pogroms; Polish, East German, Ukrainian, Yugoslav and Hungarian refugees from Nazi and Communist tyranny; Irish and Commonwealth immigrants in search of a more prosperous future in an industrial area with overfull employment. Their children and grandchildren speak with a West Riding accent and use dialect words as readily as the descendants of the Angles and the Vikings. They go *chumping* for bonfire wood, and, in true Yorkshire style, tie door knockers together and take gates off their posts on Mischief Night, 4th November, when, in 1605, mischief was brewing in London: Guy Fawkes was a 'tyke' after all). Perhaps some of them have by now, if they live in Calderdale, taken part in the annual mummery of the Pace-egging play of St George and the Dragon, which is performed in the streets on Easter Monday by schoolboys brandishing wooden swords in a portrayal of the triumph of good over evil. If they live in Calderdale they may also have tasted that local delicacy, dock leaf pudding, made for a yearly fund-raising breakfast. They will doubtless have had Bonfire Night parkin (ginger cake) and perhaps have learned to enjoy cheese with their Christmas cake and to appreciate Yorkshire pudding, served by the true Yorkshire housewife, not as an adjunct of roast beef, but as a first course, on its own with gravy. Some households, however, regard it so highly that it is served, like chips, with everything from turkey to sausage roll. The West Riding has a good claim to having been the birth-place of the English fish and chip shop, one of the earliest of which was in mid-Victorian Greenfield. Today the county has the largest in the country – Harry Ramsden's at Guiseley. Coach parties on their way home to Leeds and Bradford from a day in the Dales queue up quite happily in order to eat under the crystal chandeliers of the thickly carpeted fish restaurant, where, in a year, over a million customers eat 400,000 pounds of fish and 900,000 pounds of chips, fried in 150,000 pounds of dripping, and seasoned with 2,000 pounds of salt, 9,000 pints of vinegar and the contents of 20,000 bottles of sauce.

In late May, the words 'Chats tonight' appear on chip shop windows. It is not an invitation to the confessional but an advertisement for tiny new potatoes which are fried whole in their skins. Another feature of the Yorkshire diet are fish bits, fragmentary pieces of batter served on request with fish and chips and evidence of Yorkshire thrift; in Lancashire they are said to be thrown away. As well as fish shops there are pie shops, and while when Lancashiremen celebrate winning a darts or bowls championship they like to have a hot-pot sup-per, Yorkshiremen sup on pork pie and peas, something that can be obtained in almost every town centre pub on a weekday

1.   In the limestone country: looking down on Cray, upper Wharfedale.

lunchtime. But lately the Yorkshire palate has also developed a taste for *samosa* (rather like a highly spiced Cornish pasty), *vindaloo* and *chappatis*. The newcomers' customs have added their own flavour and interest to the Yorkshire scene. In high summer, saris among the rhododendrons combine with the red of bandsmen's uniforms in wrought-iron bandstands to make the West Riding parks seem almost like Darjeeling or Simla under the British Raj; Irish fiddlers and ballad singers entertain in the pubs; the national costumes of Eastern Europe brighten up Corpus Christi processions; and steel bands are in demand for golf club dances. Brightly coloured terraced houses (rapidly being replaced by purpose-built buildings) turn out to be Sikh temples or mosques, at least one disused Unitarian chapel has become a Polish Catholic church, and in Halifax there are two Serbian Orthodox churches in the same street – one tolerating Tito's Communist regime and the other bitterly opposed to it. And a huge Sunday afternoon congregation can regularly be seen making its way to town centre cinema showings of Indo-Pakistani love stories.

International clubs and get-togethers abound, and in 1975 Kirklees metropolitan borough held an international festival of folk culture. It would seem that the immigrant from overseas has been taken to the Yorkshireman's heart more readily than the *cummer-in* or *off-cummed-un* from another part of England, who is sometimes still treated with suspicion after ten years residence in the county. Or are the international clubs themselves run by *cummers-in*?

But the West Yorkshireman is eminently clubbable. And that is not meant simply as a reference to the abundant social clubs or the enormous and luxurious variety clubs like the Wakefield Theatre Club and the Fiesta Club in Sheffield which have set a standard for the nation in terms of comfortable mass entertainment. The tyke is more capable than most of entertaining himself, and a West Riding town seems to have more societies than a university, and certainly more than its counterpart across the Pennines. There are clubs for stamp collectors and coin collectors, for local historians and for geographers, even for bus collectors. In 1828, Barnsley had a

2. & 3. *above* Norman doorways: *left* Adel church, Leeds; *right* Selby Abbey. 4. *below* The Cloisters, Kirkstall Abbey.

Philosophical Society; today, although the mining towns are said to have less of a cultural life than the textile areas, there is a Barnsley Debating Society, a Barnsley Playgoers' Society, and a Barnsley Accordion Club. Drama, literature and music have a large following among the hard-working, hard-playing Yorkshire folk. The Thespians, the authors' circle and the choral society all play an important part in both the cultural and social life of a number of Yorkshire towns, and even small places are likely to have their own symphony orchestra, not to mention their brass band (Slaithwaite for example has both). The oldest choral society is at Halifax; perhaps the first Yorkshire brass band was that founded at Rothwell in 1838, six years after the first in the country started at Blaina in Gwent. Today the names of Yorkshire's champion town and works bands are nationally known – the Brighouse and Rastrick, John Foster's Black Dyke Mills, Hammond's Sauce Works, Grimethorpe Colliery. Churches and chapels sponsor amateur operatic societies, and dancing is another passion. Devotees of television's *Come Dancing* will be well aware that Yorkshire dancers and judges make frequent appearances. Rotherham has one of the country's few residential ballet schools, and elsewhere children, especially girls, start lessons in national and ballroom dancing at two or three years old. And when it comes to competitions they are as confident and competent as their Welsh counterparts are in their singing and recitation. The West Riding does in fact have its own equivalent *eisteddfodau* – contests for children with talent for instrumental music, recitation and song, of which the best known is probably the annual Mrs Sunderland Competition, named after Susan Sykes, soloist of the Huddersfield Choral Society to whom Queen Victoria said, 'I am Queen of England, but you are queen of song.' Leeds has its world famous international piano competition, and Settle is the smallest town in the country with a week-long drama festival, while many towns have art societies which put on annual exhibitions of members' works, and Pennine and dales villages often have galleries offering the work of local artists for sale.

Sport too plays an important part in Yorkshire life. There

are 13 professional Rugby League clubs in the Riding, and Leeds United is pre-eminent among its nine English League soccer teams, while the county cricket team has won the championship more times than any other. Yorkshiremen seem to prefer playing to watching. Nearly every village has its own football and cricket teams, and there are frequent complaints of low gates at first class matches, one reason perhaps why Huddersfield Town football club, in the first division in 1972, is, at the time of writing, in the fourth. Archery is becoming more and more popular these days among the folk who live in the textile valleys and sailing is growing in popularity too, either on the flashes which have resulted from land subsidence in the mining areas or on some of the many Pennine reservoirs originally constructed to provide compensation waters for canal locks or to supply water to the industrial towns for factory and domestic consumption. Two of this second sort of reservoir were constructed at Longwood as long ago as 1827 and 1828; also, during the planning of the M.62 trans-Pennine motorway, it was decided to build, at nearby Scammonden, a 240-foot-high dam which would not only hold back the waters of a big new reservoir but also carry the road, with the result that motorists on that highest of our motorways can enjoy both the natural beauty of the spectacular moorland scenery and the sight of coloured sails on Scammonden Water. Canal boating has brought life and colour to disused wharves in downtown districts. Anglers increasingly resort to the reservoirs, canals and rivers as man slowly wins his fight against pollution and even rivers in industrial areas like the Colne are stocked with fish. Three exhausted gravel pits on the outskirts of Brighouse have been linked together to form Cromwell Lake, a 35-acre stretch of water newly stocked with thousands of rainbow trout. The county's catch also includes dace, barbel, perch, pike, grayling, bullhead, pope, bleak, and humble stickleback, as well as lampreys and eels. And one Sunday in November crowds gather on the bridge over the Ribble on the Paythorne road, north of Gisburn, to watch the salmon go up river to spawn. The Ribble is just one of the county's major rivers, all of which have good stretches of fishing. It flows south and then west, but most flow eastwards from the Pennines to meet the Ouse in the Vale of York, and their waters then find their way to the sea by way of the Humber estuary.

Hiking is another out-door activity for which the Riding offers excellent facilities, and what splendid country there is to hike in! Perhaps the best known walker's route is the Pennine Way, a signposted walk over miles of moors. The limestone country which the Way crosses at the northern end of the Riding offers Leeds and Bradford men, getting away from the noise and fumes of the city, the opportunity to scale its crags while their sons explore its potholes and caverns. And nearer home, on the south side of lower Wharfedale, in the gritstone country, is the windy expanse of Ilkley Moor, the *Ilkla Moor* of the Yorkshire anthem.

There are only ten national parks in the country but the Dales Park is not the only one in the area of the old West Riding. For good measure there is an officially designated area of outstanding natural beauty just to the west in Bowland, a Pennine Park is planned for the Brontë country to the south, and further south still is Sheffield's playground, the Peak District National Park. Although generally associated with Derbyshire, its boundaries, marked at the roadside by huge millstones, cross those of South and West Yorkshire. A scheme has been proposed for building a miniature Aviemore, complete with hotel, cinema and ski slope in the Harden Moss area of the park, nationally known for its annual sheepdog trials and sheep shearing competition, but this would surely be an abuse of the true recreational purpose of a national park. The scheme is that of a company with shooting rights in the area. There are wide expanses of grouse moor in the Riding, and as befits a county which contained the royal forest of Bowland and Robin Hood's Barnsdale Forest, it is still very much hunting country. The list of hunts seems endless; the Rockwood, the Badsworth, the Colne Valley Beagles and the Penistone Harriers are just a few. The history of the last can be traced all the way back to 1260, while placenames in Calderdale and Kirklees remind us of the animals hunted by the Norman lords – Roebucks, Buckstones, Deerstones and Doestones, Wolfstones and

Wool(wolf)dale, and Wilber(wild boar)lee.

In this racing county, where major courses can be found all along the route of the old Great North Road at Doncaster, Pontefract, Wetherby and Ripon, the Yorkshire miner generally lets his greyhound chase an electric hare rather than a real one and races pigeons rather than shooting them, and there are many in the Riding who wish to preserve wild life, not destroy it. The first bird sanctuary in England was established last century at Walton Hall Park near Wakefield by its owner, Charles Waterton, an expert taxidermist, part of whose collection of birds and animals is in Wakefield museum. His park is no longer a bird sanctuary but the home of a water ski club. However, there is a twentieth-century sanctuary not far away on a 690-acre colliery flash called Fairburn Ings, between Kippax and Ledsham.

With voluntary labour, neighbouring slag heaps have been planted with over 10,000 trees, and a hide has been built from which 15 people can watch swans, mallard and teal on the lake. During 1971 more than 170 different species of bird were recorded here. In Autumn the Ings is visited by migrating swallows and sand-martins, sometimes a quarter of a million birds at once. Of course many reservoirs and flashes attract migratory birds, and designated reserves are by no means the only places frequented by bird watchers. On one May day in Bowland, in the five miles between Whitewell and New Hey Fell, 389 birds of 45 species were observed, including buzzard, merlin, kingfisher, dipper, twite, redshank, redstart. ring ouzel, green woodpecker and redpoll. And most industrial towns hold some attraction for the nature lover. Kestrels have been known to nest on Leeds Town Hall and collared doves are fed by children in their school yards. And when the churchyard at Lockwood, in the Holme valley south of Huddersfield, was taken over by the local council to be turned into an amenity area, part of the overgrown cemetery was kept in its natural state as a bird sanctuary. This small copse, close to the mills, is the haunt of hedge-sparrows, jays, willow warblers, coal-tits, bullfinches, greenfinches and the lesser spotted woodpecker. Just across the valley in Beaumont Park, where a disused railway track has become a nature trail, the red squirrel has its drey not far from the children's swings and paddling pool, for here, where the hills separate well-populated areas which would be unbroken save for artificial boundaries in lower lying districts, the country comes into town.

Green fields can be seen from the centres of large towns like Halifax and Huddersfield, and many of them support cattle, for this is an area Unigate has not yet conquered, an area where the small dairyman can still make a living. Foxes haunt the mill villages of Calderdale, just one representative of several species of wild animal which still survive in the Riding, ranging in size from the pigmy shrew to the red deer. Some of them are rare, like the lesser horseshoe bat, which has been sighted at Emley, and the pine marten, which has been shot(!) near Wakefield. Buckden Moor, 1,750 feet above sea level, is the site of the highest badger set in England. The badger is one of the oldest species of English mammal. In comparatively recent years the number of species in the Riding has been increased through immigration. The mountain hare was introduced into the Marsden area for hunting purposes last century, the grey squirrel has invaded the suburbs of Doncaster and Sheffield, and mink, escaping from fur farms, have proved a menace to poultry in the Elland district, while escaped chipmunk have been found near Leeds. Some of the county's grass-snakes are escaped pets and of continental origin, but there are large numbers of the native variety in the drained marshlands of the Doncaster area. The adder is common too on the drier moors, but varieties of reptile are few. The common toad turns up in suburban gardens, and small boys still catch tadpoles and newts. Those who prefer butterflies can find the rare large heath butterfly on the Thorne and Hatfield marshes, though one hopes they will leave it alone. The insect life of the Riding deserves a book to itself, it is so varied. This is due to the variations in scenery and weather. Another of those pit flashes which have become nature reserves, Denaby Ings, is particularly noted for its insect life. Some insects belong to the Arctic-Alpine species which flourished in the cold conditions that followed in the wake of retreating Ice Age glaciers. These include the sawfly *pontania collactanea,* whose bright red galls can be found on the leaves of trees around Malham Tarn. The country is also rich in molluscs; 30 different species of snail have been identified in a ditch at Thorner.

For those who prefer flowers to animal life the West Riding is a happy hunting ground, once again because of its complex geological structure. In the Pennines, pink birdseye primrose, blue jacob's ladder, yellow mountain pansy, and purple saxifrage grow on the limestone cliffs and slopes. Bilberry (its fruit a favourite pie-filler), cloudberry, cowberry and cranberry can be found where gritstone rocks (alternate sandstone and shale forming shelves called slacks) are near the surface. In the boggier places little grows besides peat-based cotton grass, but there is some heather, the chief food of the grouse, in the better drained parts. One of the most delightful flowers of the gritstone district is the autumn crocus which carpets the fields around Halifax with purple in late September and early October, while in springtime the darkest corners of the local woods of oak, birch and mountain ash are bright with bluebells. On the magnesium limestone belt, which runs parallel to the Pennines further east, grow the rock rose, burnet rose, purple milk vetch and wild liquorice, while the marshlands of Thorne Moor and Hatfield Chase are the home of the rare bog rosemary. In some places an effort is being made to preserve rare flora. and in, for example, Cross Wood near Grassington, where there are 300 varieties of wild flower, picking is definitely discouraged. There are also many places near to the built-up areas where the naturalist can indulge in his hobby without restriction, particularly the rich woodlands of the South Yorkshire coal measures, between the Pennines and the magnesium ridge, where there are oases of beauty within a mile or two of every pit-head. Indeed, although it was best known for its moors, its mines and its mills, the former West Riding, half of which was officially classified as an agricultural zone, contained not only a population of three and a half million people, but a great variety of scenery from mountain and valley in the west to level plain and marsh in the east, and was, without a doubt, one of the loveliest counties in Britain, as well as one of the most rich in history.

The region is full of monuments of the past. There is a Middle Stone Age site, where schoolboys can still pick up the odd flint arrowhead, near Marsden, a Bronze Age stone circle at Yockenthwaite, and an Iron Age farm near Meltham. There are traces of Roman forts in several places, including one inside another at Castleshaw, and the foundations of a complete Roman town at Aldborough. There is Anglo-Saxon work in the churches at Ledsham, Bardsey and elsewhere, and there are over 150 Anglian and Scandinavian carved stones, including hog-back gravestones and crosses, while Norman church buildings are legion, particularly in the Vale of York, which, being a low-lying and marshy area, early man had avoided, and which William I is said to have devastated, and where, consequently, there are few earlier monuments. The Conqueror divided England between his barons and the castles of William de Romillé at Skipton, Gilbert Tison at Knaresborough, Ilbert de Lacy at Pontefract, William de Warrenne at Conisbrough, and Roger de Busli at Tickhill still stand, albeit rebuilt and sometimes less than complete. The fields where a later baronage battled or rebel Earl Thomas of Lancaster against the weak Edward II or fought out the Wars of the Roses can still be traced, as can the battlefields of the English Civil War, when the Fairfaxes, a West Riding family, commanded the Parliamentary army, Bradford was besieged by the Royalists, and Charles I received his most telling defeat on Marston Moor.

Here too are the remains of great monastic houses like those of the Cistercians at Fountains, Kirkstall and Roche, and mansions like Fountains Hall and Nostell Priory, built after the monasteries had been dissolved by Henry VIII, on the monks' lands and sometimes with the monks' stones. Although some, like Whitley Beaumont, have been swept away, the West Riding abounds in great houses, most no longer lived in by the great families, who have retreated as the smoke of industry has advanced. Bretton Hall, seat of the Wentworths and the Beaumonts, is a college of education and Woodsome Hall, seat of the Kayes and the Legges, is, like a dozen others, a golf club.

Some great houses are now museums, but the Lascelles still live at Harewood and the Ingilbys at Ripley, both well away from the smoke. There are many lesser country houses too, some now run as hotels, other reduced in status from manor house to farm.

But perhaps the most impressive monuments from the past are not those of the monks, the feudal lords or the gentry, but those contributed to the West Riding scene by industry – the mills, the mines and the steel works; the impressive pieces of engineering, like the Bingley Five Rise locks, on the canals built to carry their products; the port of Goole, 50 miles from the sea and new in 1826, and the new town of Saltaire, built to house the workers in Sir Titus Salt's mohair factory; the railways, the canals' successors, with their own monumental architecture, like the great viaducts on the Settle-Carlisle line and on the way into Harrogate from Leeds; the impressive town centres of Huddersfield, Keighley and Halifax, and the proud town halls of Halifax, Bradford and Morley, all built with the wealth industry created; and the grand churches built by the manufacturers in their own memory. Industry created many of the features of the West Riding scene, bad as well as good – the lead spoil heaps of the Dales and the coal and iron spoil heaps of South Yorkshire; the back-to-back houses, one up, one down and a cellar-head kitchen, with one earth closet between two; the people's parks that provided an escape from them. All these things make the West Riding an absorbing field of research for the industrial archaeologist and the social historian.

The spas for which the county was once famous – Holbeck, Lockwood, Ossett, Slaithwaite and Askern, Boston, Ilkley and Harrogate – were long ago invaded by industry or have more recently ceased to be economically viable, and the Riding has no coastline, but it is an area so well-endowed with beauty and historical interest that it well repays investigation by that fast-growing band of people who wisely avoid the crowded beaches of Ibiza and Majorca, the Costa Brava and the Costa del Sol, and seek the rewards to be gained from exploring on their own doorstep – not least the Yorkshireman himself.

CHAPTER ONE

The Plain — Selby and Boothferry

York, the North's number one tourist city, whose handsome railway station must be one of very few in England to have a Way Out sign written in four languages, belonged to none of the ridings, though in a sense to all of them. Situated where the three ridings met, it was a county in itself with its own sheriff and assizes, but now the city is a mere district of the new county of North Yorkshire. To the south lies another – the Selby district, bounded on the west by the low ridge of magnesium limestone where the Romans built the forerunner of the A.1, and on the east by the river Derwent. The area between the ridge and the river Ouse was once in the West Riding, the rest in the East Riding. In the Ice Age all this land was covered by a glacier and when the ice cap melted it left behind a vast lake known to geologists as Lake Humber. In time the waters of the lake found an outlet to the sea but the area they had covered remained wet and swampy, long to be avoided by man. As late as the twelfth century A.D. the region was described as one of swamp and thick forest. But by then much land had already been reclaimed and settlements had been made in what, through persistent effort, was to become one of the richest farming areas in the country. Today the Balne area in the southern part of the district is well known among farmers and brewers for its prize-winning malting barley.

There is a tradition that the Romans were the first to find the hard water in the limestone country ideal for brewing when they had a camp at *Calcaria* on one of their military roads to the legionary fortress at York. Certainly they sunk some of the

wells which are used by brewers in present-day *Calcaria*, Tadcaster, for their water supply. But the earliest chronicled reference to brew-houses in the town dates from 1341, when one
paid 8d in tax and another 4d. In 1378 Tadcaster had five
registered innkeepers, and even now the buildings which make
the biggest impression on someone passing through the town
are the numerous public houses and the huge yellowy-white
stone brewery topped with the slogan 'Magnet Ales brewed
here'. There are not as many inns now as there were in the days
when Tadcaster was an important coaching station on the road
from York to Leeds. Some have been demolished, the Angel is
two shops, and the Golden Lion in Bridge Street, used by stage
waggons, the 'slow coaches' which carried goods and those
who could not afford to travel any better, is the office of
brewery architects. But the White Swan survives and so does
the Londesborough, which, as the White Horse, was Tadcaster's leading coaching inn. In the late eighteenth century it was
owned by William Backhouse, who horsed four of the eight
London stage coaches which passed through the town every
day. The local postmaster, John Hartley, used the Rose and
Crown as a change house for mail coaches, and also horsed the
Leeds to Scarborough coach. In 1758 Hartley and Backhouse
went into partnership as brewers in premises behind the White
Horse. In 1847, at a time when Tadcaster was suffering from a
depression due to the effect of railway transport on the coaching trade, the brewery was taken over by one John Smith, who
rebuilt the business by concentrating on producing a clear beer
for marketing all over Yorkshire. When Smith died, his
brothers William and Samuel took over, but there was a family
quarrel and after Samuel's death William moved the business
to the brewery which dominates the town today, leaving
Samuel's son, another Samuel, with an empty building. But
the young man shared the determination and business acumen
of the rest of the family and restarted brewing at the old
brewery, with the result that today there are two firms with
descendants of the original John Smith on the board giving the
air of Tadcaster its all-pervading sickly-sweet scent. And
throughout the West Riding, wherever there is a John Smith's

house under the sign of the magnet, there is usually a Sam Smith's house nearby, perhaps even next-door, displaying the white rose of York and boasting that its ales come from Yorkshire's oldest brewery.

Coal mining seems to be bidding fair to become the most important industry in the Vale of York as plans go ahead for the exploitation of what is potentially the most productive coalfield in Europe. There is, however, another extractive industry with roots at least as deep as those of the brewing trade – quarrying. The Romans built *Calcaria* from local stone, and the Vavasours of Hazlewood, four miles away, gave stone from their quarry for the building of York Minster.

The palace of the archbishops of York is at Bishopthorpe on the banks of the Ouse. And in these days when bishops are tending more and more to choose to live in small detached houses in suburbia, Bishopthorpe really does seem palatial. Its foundations were laid on the instructions of Archbishop Grey in the thirteenth century, but today it has the appearance of an eighteenth-century country house, its gatehouse and main façade having been built in the style known as Strawberry Hill Gothick by Archbishop Drummond in the 1760s.

Drummond rebuilt Bishopthorpe with the stone from another archiepiscopal palace at Cawood further down river, where all that remains now is a fourteenth-century gatehouse wedged between a brick farmhouse and a barn. Yet this was once the haunt of kings. John came here to hunt, and his son Henry III came with a retinue of a 1,000 knights to meet his homesick daughter Margaret and her husband Alexander of Scotland. Edward I wintered here during one of his Scottish campaigns. With him was his second wife, another Margaret, who gave birth to their son Thomas not far away at Brotherton on the banks of the Aire. Edward II stayed here too, while raising the army which was to lose to the Scots at Bannockburn.

Thomas Wolsey, cardinal archbishop of York, came here in disgrace in 1530, having failed to procure a papal annulment of Henry VIII's marriage to Catherine of Aragon. He described the short time he spent at Cawood as the happiest days of his life, and he managed to win the affection of the flock he had long neglected while he had been engaged in state business as chancellor. But he had earned the hatred of the new queen, Anne Boleyn, and on the day before he was due to be enthroned, the earl of Northumberland came to arrest him for high treason. He died at Leicester, on his way to London, and thus escaped the headsman's axe. It is said that Wolsey planned to make Cawood into a second Hampton Court, but he only had time to make repairs to the existing house. Later archbishops preferred to live at Bishopthorpe, and in 1646, after it had been held by the Royalists as an outpost of their Civil War defences of York city, Cawood Castle was captured by Parliamentary troops and dismantled.

The archbishops had yet another palace at Sherburn-in-Elmet, given to them, as had been Cawood, by the Anglo-Saxon king Athelstan, after he had taken the area from the Danes, but nothing can be seen of it now, apart from a few lumps in a field north of the church. Sherburn church stands on a green hill in what is almost a separate 'church town', away from the long, untidy village of inns and social clubs, petrol stations, old stone farms and modern brick shops which straggles along part of the main A.162 road from Ferrybridge to Tadcaster. Its white Perpendicular tower seems to dominate the landscape, and the impression one gets approaching the building is of a big fifteenth-century village church with a chancel with three thin lancet windows which might be earlier than the rest or might be Victorian. One is quite unprepared for what lies inside – a splendid Norman nave with massive round pillars which lean out of true, towards the aisles. Like many parish churches, Sherburn's is a composite of the work of several centuries, and each age's contribution has been clearly labelled for the instruction of the visitor. One sign reads: *All Hallows Church. 15th Century. The Clerestory built over the knave (sic)*. All, apart from the east wall of the chancel, which is in fact Victorian, and unfortunately plastered, is in the clean white stone of the area. Apart from a light and potentially very attractive Tudor chapel which is used as a broom cupboard, the building is well cared for, and the treasures from its long past are well preserved. Particularly impressive is the gravestone of a medieval priest, carved with cross, book and chalice, which lies under the eastern arch of the tower.

Sherburn church is only one of several in the district to contain Norman work within its walls. Cawood, for example, has a Norman doorway and there is a Norman arch at Tadcaster, while Brayton has a Norman nave and south doorway, and a Norman tower which was crowned with a octagonal stage and spire in the fifteenth century. Indeed there can be few areas of England richer in relics of Norman days than the Vale of York. One could spend a very enjoyable few days walking through its pleasant countryside from ancient church to ancient church, or one might prefer to use a bike. This level plain is still very much cyclists' country. The biggest shop in the village of South Milford, which has not many, is a cycle shop, and the present Archbishop of York rides a bike.

The greatest church of the area, rich in the relics of many centuries and displaying examples of each style of architecture from Norman to perpendicular, is Selby Abbey. Its first abbot was Benedict, a monk from Auxerre in France, who is said to have been sent to Selby in 1069 by St German, a 5th-century bishop of Auxerre, who appeared to him in a vision. At least that is the story told in a history of the abbey written by a twelfth-century monk. Recent theories are that William the Conqueror founded the monastery as an act of expiation for his sin in being involved in a poisoning; that he did so as a thank-offering for the birth of his son, the future Henry I, probably born at Selby in 1068; and that he wanted a small colony of men loyal to him in an area of considerable resistance to his rule.

Whatever the cause of its foundation, the great Norman church of Selby still stands. In 1969 it celebrated 900 years of its existence with a visit from the Queen, who distributed the Royal Maundy there. It was the first time that had happened in a parish church, for that is what the abbey has been since 1618, the monastery having been dissolved, like all the others, by Henry VIII. Nine hundred souvenir plates were made by the Spode China Company, and one can be seen in a case in the south transept of the church, alongside the signatures of the Queen and other visiting dignitaries, and samples of maundy money. The plates bear the arms of the abbey, which depict the swans that, according to legend, led Benedict up the Ouse to Selby.

From the direction of the railway station, the abbey is approached across a pleasant green which has as its centrepiece the old market cross of 1775. The most striking thing about the building is its length – 100 yards. It looks like a cathedral in miniature, built carefully to scale, and to add to the illusion that it is not quite the real thing, its stonework is gleaming white. On near inspection some parts of the recently cleaned church seem cleaner than others, indeed almost new, and in fact they are. The central tower fell down in 1690, as a result of neglect by the lords of the manor who were responsible for its upkeep, and it brought the south transept down with it. The tower was rebuilt but in 1906, another date like 1690 with the same combination of numbers as the year of the abbey's foundation, 1096, a disastrous fire swept through the church. (A further disaster was half-expected in 1960, but nothing extraordinary happened.) After the fire, major reconstruction work began. The central tower was again rebuilt, a new south transept was added, and in 1935 the two west towers were raised one storey and given parapets to match those of the central tower, while statues of King George V and Queen Mary and of the then archbishops of Canterbury and York were erected to flank the Norman west doorway.

The nave of alternate round and compound pillars, is perhaps the most impressive part of the church. It is Norman work begun in the time of the second abbot, Hugh, who ruled the monastery from 1097 to 1123. One of the round pillars on the south side of the nave is named after him. It bears a criss-cross pattern known as reticulated moulding, and the similarity between the work here and that in the nave of Durham cathedral suggests that both may have been designed by the same architect. Above the nave arches is the triforium, a long arcaded gallery, Norman and Transitional in style on the north side and partly Early English on the south. Higher still are the windows of the Early English clerestory. The choir, in the more elaborate Decorated style, was begun in 1280, and replaced a shorter one of Abbot Hugh's day. The church's great east window is a wonderful piece of stained glass, dating in part from 1340, with a huge figure of Jesse at the bottom and a vine-like tree rising from him and embracing his descendants, with Mary and the child Jesus in the topmost branches.

Behind the altar and outside the screen round the choir is a processional way called an ambulatory. Its outer walls are arcaded, and the pillars of the arcades have marvellous capitals, some original medieval work, and some carved after the 1906 fire. Those in the south ambulatory feature pigs eating acorns, fishes among seaweed, a cock and a hen, and birds eating berries. One in the north ambulatory is hollow, and if you look through its carved leaves you can see a tiny bust of Edward VII. Close by is a great square shaft or squint which might at one time have allowed lepers outside the church to see mass being celebrated at the high altar. Now the view of the altar is obscured by the choir screen, and the other end of the squint is not outside the church but in the sacristy. Once a chantry chapel, the sacristy is an example of yet another style of English medieval architecture, Perpendicular. The old sacristy, on the other side of the church, is now the war memorial chapel. A room above it, once the monks' scriptorium or writing room, was in the eighteenth and nineteenth centuries used as a blue-coat school.

There is practically nothing left of the secular buildings of the abbey, but the town itself, although partly settled before Benedict's arrival, is a monument to the days when the monks controlled its fortunes. The street name Bondgate possibly indicates that that was where the abbot's villeins or bondmen lived, and his mill was in Millgate. Life centred on the abbey. Many of Selby's citizens were its tenants, the abbot's court administered local government and meted out justice to lawbreakers. And the market was held in the churchyard until, in 1324, the archbishop forbade this and it was moved to the present Market Place.

There is another square in Selby – Micklegate or Wide

5. & 6.   *above* Ripon Cathedral; *below* Fountains Abbey and the River Skell.

Street, where every year in November the Martinmas Fair is held, but of the town which existed when Selby first got its charters for market and fair hardly anything remains. There are no medieval houses still standing, although in Church Lane traces have been found of several medieval shops or booths. On the left-hand side of the lane as one approaches the abbey are some old people's bed-sitters, cheaply built in brick, but more pleasing than they might otherwise have been for being roofed with red pantiles in the local style. In 1973, before they were put up, their site was investigated by archaeologists who found the remains of what had obviously been a fourteenth-century cobbler's shop. In a hole where he had dumped his waste leather were found a child's bootee and a dagger sheaf marked with a fleur-de-lys. Also found on the site were a silver long-cross penny of the reign of Edward III and a lead seal bearing the name of the cobbler himself, Martin Williamson. By checking the abbey records it was possible for the archaeologists to discover the exact time when he lived in the house and the names of his next-door neighbours.

At the end of Micklegate, near to the river, is another relic of medieval Selby – a large warehouse, the older parts of which are built of magnesium limestone blocks. Known as the Abbot's Staith, it is evidence of Selby's importance as a port in the later Middle Ages. Above Selby the river was subject to silting and was obstructed by weirs to aid fishing, so it was here that goods were transferred from large seagoing vessels to the smaller river craft which could negotiate these hazards. In the fifteenth century Selby was already a shipbuilding centre. One of the vessels used to take Henry V's men to Normandy on the Agincourt campaign was the *Catherine* of Selby, and later in the century, Selby-built ships regularly sailed to the Netherlands on behalf of York and Hull merchants. Selby yards still build ships, notably trawlers, which are launched sideways into the river. The town's fortunes as a port suffered in the early years of the eighteenth century when 'improvements' to the channels of the Ouse's tributaries, the Aire and its tributary the Calder, provided Leeds and the textile area beyond with their own navigable waterway to the Humber, by-passing Selby. Things

7.   Brimham Rocks, Nidderdale.

began to get better in 1778 when a five-mile canal was constructed between Selby and the Aire's lowest lock at Huddlesey. To draw business to the revitalised port, the wooden forerunner of the present Selby swing bridge was built, providing a connection by road with the East Riding. Woollens were brought from the new West Riding mills by canal and loaded on to bigger boats. By 1800 370,000 tons of goods were being handled annually, and in 1815 the introduction of a steam packet service on the Ouse made Selby a passenger port with steamers operating between the town and York, Hull and even London.

The new prosperity produced a small class of 'merchant princes', of whom the most influential were members of the Audus family. In 1830 James Audus owned 18 schooners which sailed regularly to London, and he used some of the wealth they made him for the good of Selby. He endowed charities, and in 1866 built St James' church at the end of Audus Street. It once had a spire but this was demolished on 10 May 1944 when a British aircraft engaged in night-flying crashed into it. Houses nearby were damaged and 11 people were killed.

It was Audus who brought the railway to Selby. That was in 1834, a time when the rival port of Goole was being developed at the end of a new branch of the Aire and Calder Navigation further downstream, and the merchants of Selby were anxious to keep their control over the shipment of West Riding textiles. But Goole itself had a rail link with the textile belt by 1848, and the mid-Victorian period was a time of stagnation in Selby. Between 1841 and 1861 the population stabilized at approximately 5,500 and only the arrival of 500 Irish labourers in the aftermath of the potato famine prevented a sharp decline. The Petre family, the lords of the manor, who were themselves Roman Catholics, built the new church of St Mary for them, and today 40 per cent of the people of Selby are Roman Catholic.

But Selby had obvious advantages as a route centre and the town has regained some of its former prosperity. Seagoing ships, particularly of Dutch and German origin, still load and unload their cargoes at its wharves which are at the natural limit of navigation for ships of modern coaster size (500 tons). Many of them bring grain to the tall flour mills on the waterfront. Besides flour, mustard is milled here, bacon is processed and synthetic dyes are produced. There is, therefore, still a link with the textile area further west. Actually, for a long time Selby was itself an important cloth manufacturing centre. One of the earliest records we have of this aspect of the town's activities is of 1274, when Selby weavers were accused of producing cloth of inferior quality. A guide book of 1835 refers to the firm of Dobson and Co., worsted manufacturers, and there was a flax mill in the town until 1936.

Besides its associations with cloth, Selby shares another interest with the Pennine valleys of the West Riding – a long-standing love of music. In a case on the wall of the south aisle of the abbey nave is an example of that indispensable ingredient of the early nineteenth-century church choir and orchestra, the leather serpent. A notice records that it was played by Mr Robinson in a musical festival held in the abbey in 1827, when the *Messiah* was performed. I was in the church on a Saturday afternoon in December 1974 and the Selby Choral Society were rehearsing Fauré's *Requiem*, while outside, in the Market Place, the Abbey Handbellringers were playing Christmas carols. The lights were lit on the Christmas tree, but there was blossom on the trees in the old cholera graveyard on the north side of the church, and a few hundred yards away in the Quaker burial-ground roses were scenting the air of that particularly mild December. The Quaker burial-ground has been there since 1692, but apart from there being a few graveslabs brought there from another cemetery at Drax Abbey Farm, it looks like the front garden of a lazy suburban householder – a bed of roses surrounded by concrete flags. The old meeting house was till recently a café and is now a supermarket. Another, even more valuable relic of Selby's past, the medieval abbey tithe barn in James Street, was allowed to fall into ruin, and its remains were incorporated into what was a discotheque and is now a bingo hall.

Among the people who paid tithes to the abbey were the

inhabitants of Monk Fryston, about seven miles west of Selby. It got the Monk part of its name when it was given to the abbey by the archbishop of York. It is a village full of surprises, the element of surprise heightened by the twists in the road through it; one does not know what to expect around the next bend. There are a number of ancient limestone houses, a once hexagonal Methodist chapel of the 1840 offering a welcome to those who 'prefer a simpler form of worship', and, something rare in these parts, a blue-washed thatched cottage by the gates of the Hall. The Hall itself, now a restaurant, though largely Victorian is also partly Tudor, and has lovely gardens and a lake. The church provides perhaps the biggest surprise of all. Its pinnacled tower can be seen from afar, and looks a fine example of the Perpendicular work of the early fifteenth century, but on close inspection it is clear that all below the blue and gold clock face is Saxon, complete with original windows. The church stands on a rise above a small green in a very trim churchyard, its trimness achieved without removing headstones, so often works of art as well as valuable aids to the social historian, and yet so often destroyed by those who think that a green lawn equals beauty. Monk Fryston is the sort of place which would blossom from the attentions of the Civic Trust, although it could end up looking a little too tidy and lose some of its character. Though the road through it is busy and fume-ridden, there is only one serious blemish on the face of this otherwise visually delightful village – a house of bright red brick, recently fitted with a bow window. Some plaster on the walls and all might be well.

Fryston's landlords were not the only religious order in the area in the Middle Ages. The military order of Knights Templar had a house at Temple Hirst. The Templars were founded to protect pilgrims on their way to and from the Holy Sepulchre in Jerusalem and were pledged to perpetual war against the infidel Moslems, with the object of turning them out of the Holy Land. They lodged in Jerusalem near the Temple, from which they took their name. Their numbers increased with each crusade, and by the middle of the twelfth century they had branch houses, called preceptories, all over Europe. The one at

Hirst was founded in 1152. With the finish of the crusades the Order fell into idleness and disrepute. Prompted in part by resentment at their arrogance and still-growing wealth, both Church and State brought charges of extremely scandalous behaviour against them. They were suppressed in England in 1308 and for a long time the knights of Temple Hirst were imprisoned in York castle, the king giving their lands to the Darcy family. The house is now a farm, but it has retained a number of its distinctive features, including an octagonal tower, said to be one of eleven which originally surrounded the core of the building.

The Vale of York has seen much of doings of knights and noblemen, some honourable and some otherwise, and a good deal of noble blood has been shed there. Thomas, earl of Lancaster, one of the West Riding's most powerful land-owners, met his supporters at Sherburn to plan a rebellion against the ill-fated Edward II, who had forsaken the counsels of great landowners like Lancaster himself for those of upstart favourites. Archbishop Scrope, involved in an insurrection against a later king, Henry IV, was tried in his own palace at Bishopthorpe and beheaded on nearby Bishop's Hill. He is said to be one of the archbishops depicted in the fifteenth-century east window of the church at Bolton Percy. It was with the Percys that he had plotted against the king. Although usually associated with Northumberland, they did not acquire their lands there until 1309. Before that their chief estates had been in Yorkshire. Bolton was in fact granted to William de Perci by the Conqueror. And Henry Percy, the third earl of Northumberland, died fighting for Henry VI not far away on the field of Towton. Towton was one of the most decisive battles of the Wars of the Roses and resulted in Edward, duke of York becoming Edward IV of England. Fought in a blinding snowstorm with the wind blowing in the Lancastrians' faces on Palm Sunday 1461, it was also perhaps the bloodiest battle fought on English soil, with an estimated 33,000 dead. Many must have been men of the West Riding, for King Henry, descendant of the rebel Earl Thomas, was duke of Lancaster and owned the vast duchy estates which covered much of the county, and they were his tenants and liegemen. The battle is commemorated by a cross at the roadside between Towton and Saxton, but some of the bloodiest fighting was near the Cock Beck, towards which the Lancastrians retreated when the duke of Norfolk appeared with Yorkist reinforcements, but which, swollen with rain and snow, they found too deep to ford. It was here that Northumberland perished, and the stream, which can be reached by a path opposite the Rockingham Arms, Towton, is said to have run red with blood for 24 hours. Scores of the dead are reputed to have been buried close to Lead church, a tiny place only 18 feet long, standing forlornly alone in a field off the B.1217. A mound marks another communal grave to the north of Saxton church, not far from the altar tomb of the Lancastrian leader Lord Dacre. Said to have been shot by a boy in a tree as he stopped to drink, there is a tradition that Dacre was buried sitting on his horse, and when his grave was opened last century an upright skeleton was found with horse bones underneath. There was not even a churchyard tomb for another Lancastrian lord – Clifford. Known as 'the Butcher' because of his conduct in the battle of Wakefield the previous year, he was killed in a skirmish the day before Towton and his body was flung into a pit with those of the common soldiers.

The Vale of York was to witness rebellion and civil war again in the two succeeding centuries. Robert Aske, leader of the Pilgrimage of Grace, a revolt which had as one of its objects preventing Henry VIII from dissolving the monasteries, made Selby his headquarters in November 1536. One of his fellow 'officers' was Lord Darcy of Temple Hirst, then chief steward of the abbey, and men from Selby, Wistow and Cawood are known to have played a violent part in the rebellion.

In the great Civil War of King *versus* Parliament fought in the 1640s, the West Riding provided two of the greatest generals on the Parliamentary side – Ferdinando, lord Fairfax, and his son Sir Thomas. They garrisoned Selby for Parliament against Charles I early in 1643, and eventually, after seeing a lot of action locally, Thomas became general-in-chief of the Parliamentary forces. But when the fighting was over and the king was on trial for treason he would have no part in the proceedings. Perhaps by this time Fairfax himself was a Royalist, or at least not too enamoured of his former subordinate Oliver Cromwell who became England's dictator. He actually plotted with General Monck, who stayed at his house at Nun Appleton, for Charles II's restoration and provided the horse which the king rode at his coronation. He died in 1671 and was buried in Bilbrough church. On his daughter's death the Appleton estate was bought by Alderman Milner of Leeds and it was his family which built the house that is there today.

Despite changes of ownership and the emergence of a new gentry who had made their money through trade, the big houses of the Yorkshire plain continued to provide officers for the armed forces when the need arose. At the roadside on the southern outskirts of South Milford stands an impressive stone cross. It commemorates Captain Frank Bryan Parker, last commander of 'D' company of the tenth battalion of the Yorkshire Regiment, who, an inscription says, served three winters in France and one in Murmansk. He was killed in action against the Bolsheviks near Archangel on Sunday, 23 March 1919. He was 22. 'D' company was disbanded because of the large number of casualties it sustained. Also commemorated on the monument are ten officers of the company and 106 of other ranks who were killed in action between 1915 and 1919. Behind the cross are the stables of Captain Parker's old home; they have been made into a motel, the Cocked Hat. The Parkers' house, red-brick, mock-Jacobean Milford Hall is a country club, evidence of a further change which has taken place in estate ownership this century.

South Milford is one of those places many people have heard of but comparatively few have seen. Long a famous railway junction, its station serves a number of the villages of the plain, so its name is often heard over the loudspeakers in Liverpool, Manchester, Leeds and Hull. And it is an interesting station. On the Leeds-Selby line, the first commercial passenger and goods line in the Riding, its booking office and waiting room are on a level with the track and not on the platform, which is a later innovation. The village is a few hundred yards down the road. It has a Low Street which, despite its lack of shops, has, with the traffic rushing through, something of the character of a high street, and it has a High Street which is more like a country lane. When the last house is left behind and the road really is a country lane, with a limestone wall on the right and elms and chestnuts lining the ditch on the left, suddenly one is back in the Middle Ages. At the top of a long green bank, among hay-filled barns and cartloads of turnips, is the impressive white stone fourteenth-century gatehouse of Steeton Hall, with chimney, gargoyles, outside staircase and a marvellous display of medieval heraldry on the corbels under its battlements. Through the gateway one can get a glimpse of Steeton Hall itself, looking rather ramshackle with the three fourteenth-century arched windows of its chapel on the ground floor.

Few other medieval domestic buildings survive in the area. There are said to be slight traces of a fifteenth-century house at Carlton-in-Balne. They are to be found in the Jacobean portion of the largely Victorian Carlton Towers, the seat of the lords Beaumont. The present lord Beaumont is Miles Fitzalan Howard, the duke of Norfolk. The barony of Beaumont is unusual in being heritable through the female line, and the duke's grandmother, one of the Stapletons of Carlton, brought it into the Howard family when she married the late lord Howard of Glossop. One of the Stapletons died at Bannockburn, another fought at Crécy and was one of the first 25 Knights of the Garter, and another was at Agincourt. Carlton has an elaborately furnished church built by them in 1863.

The southern part of the Selby district has a number of churches by well-known Victorian architects. Perhaps the most interesting are the little bellcoted church at Heck designed by Temple Moore, and the church built by William Butterfield for lord Downe at Hensall. Butterfield, who designed Keble College, Oxford and the famous London 'high' churches of All Saints', Margaret Street and St Alban's, Holborn, was probably at his best when building in brick. He used it at Hensall for church, vicarage and village school.

The eastern boundary of Hensall parish is now also the county boundary. Neighbouring Pollington and Cowick, which also have Butterfield churches and vicarages, lie in what was the Goole rural district of the West Riding, and this, with Goole borough and the East Riding rural district of Howden, was formed in 1974 into the Boothferry district of the county of Humberside. The district is named after the old ferry across the Ouse at what was to become the first bridging point upstream from the mouth of the Humber and where the M.62 now crosses the river en route from Liverpool to Hull.

The lord Downe who employed Butterfield to build the churches lived at Cowick Hall, which has been described as the best example in England of the domestic work of the eighteenth-century architect James Paine. This fine house with its dormer windows and a system of giant pilasters all the way round its outside walls is now the headquarters of a chemical company. The tombs of lord Downe's ancestors, the Dawnays, are in the parish church at Snaith. In that church's chancel floor are signs of there once having been one of the biggest monumental brasses in England. A mitred figure with a pastoral staff, it was reputedly the memorial of Robert Rogers, the last abbot of Selby, who died at Rawcliffe, a few miles east of Snaith, in 1559, 20 years after the Dissolution, and was brought here to the church of his monastery's only daughter house for burial.

The village next-door to Rawcliffe is Airmyn, a pleasant place on the banks of the Aire, just before it meets the Ouse. Between the houses, which line only one side of the village street, and the river is a green with a memorable Gothic clock tower commemorating a former lord of the manor, George Percy, earl of Beverley. The next village, Hook, is a riverside one too, its main street running parallel to the Ouse, and then comes the district's 'capital', Goole.

Despite the tree-lined approach along Boothferry Road, Goole is not at first sight a very prepossessing place. Its streets of brick terraced houses look as if they had been picked up from the heart of industrial Lancashire by some giant crane and dumped here in an alien countryside, and the town's shopping centre is torn in two by a busy railway line. But turn off the main road into Aire Street and one is in a different world. Here are tall, once elegant, early nineteenth-century terraces, three storeys high and distinguished by the gracefully rounded corners which end each block, incorporating the doorway of a shop or a pub. Regrettably, with their boarded-up windows, they look as if they have not long to go before they fall victim to the demolition men. Only one block is reasonably intact. In the middle of it is an unexpected sight, a flag-poled office bearing the badges of the Danish and Belgian vice-consulates. For Aire Street is the original main street of the port of Goole created by the Aire and Calder Navigation Company in 1826, and at the end of it is a bridge which swings open to let the big ships through into docks 50 miles from the North Sea. One of the best things about Goole is that the docks are accessible to you and me. We can wonder about unchallenged, watching ships bringing ore for Sheffield steel from Scandinavia or timber from Russia come into port from the Ouse through the great Ocean Lock. And we can see Renault cars being unloaded from the bowels of an Auto Liner in the Ouse Dock, or tug-pulled containers shaped like huge baking tins and called Tom Puddings, which are brought here in a long train along the canal, being hauled up from the water by a hoist and then tipped up to let their contents, best Yorkshire coal or coke, fall into the hold of a ship bound perhaps for Germany or France.

Towering above the scene is the tall black spire of St John's church, built by the Navigation Company in 1843, with its memorials to Goole men and ships lost at sea. Older than the church is the Lowther Hotel, hard by the Aire Street swing bridge, where the official feast was held on the day the port opened. It was once the Banks Arms, having been built at the expense of Sir Edward Banks, of Joliffe and Banks, principal contractors for the port works. When Sir Edward died, the Navigation Company bought it and renamed it the Lowther, after the company chairman, Sir John Lowther.

Although most of the original town has disappeared as the docks have been extended, a number of public houses remain even in their busiest parts. Foreign seamen seem to like English beer and the English girls they meet when they are drinking it.

At the end of Bridge Street is the Verminden. It is named after Cornelius Vermuyden, nephew of the Dutch ambassador to the court of Charles I, who was commissioned to drain the vast south Yorkshire marshes. By building embankments to prevent the river Don from flooding the land, he made the northern channel of the river, which he diverted to join the Aire instead of the Ouse, take more water than either it or the Aire could properly hold, with the result that instead of stopping floods he caused a disastrous one in the region of Snaith, Sykehouse and Fishlake, and to remedy matters had to make a new river bed from Snaith to Goole. This was the Dutch River, which the Verminden overlooks, and it cost him £20,000.

Leaving the port by the bridge over the Dutch River, the A.161 passes by the yard of the Goole Shipbuilding and Repair Company on its way to Swinefleet. Here King Canute's father, Sweyn Forkbeard is thought to have landed in 1013. From Swinefleet one may take the road towards what was once north Lincolnshire but is now South Humberside through fertile cornfields created from a black goose-feeding marsh by 'warping'. This process, now seldom if ever practised, involved the leading of water from the Ouse on to the fields through sluices at high tide, and then letting it drain away with the tide to leave a deposit of silt which in two to three years would become a rich topsoil. The silt was formed from boulder clay eroded from the Holderness cliff at the mouth of the Humber. The land around here is as flat as a pancake, so that the spire of the Lincolnshire church of Luddington, which is no giant, can be seen from miles around. It is windmill and pantile country, which, although the windmills have lost their sails, has reminded many visitors of Holland. One attractive village, Eastoft, with a beautifully cared for, richly carpeted, Victorian church, whose cheerful caretaker keeps the key in her cottage across the road, was till 1974 half in Lincolnshire and half in the West Riding. The boundary was the old channel of the Don, still traceable between church and cottage.

On another road out of Swinefleet is Whitgift church, seemingly below the level of the Ouse whose broad waters are held back by a huge embankment where the monks of Selby abbey built a sea wall to protect their lands as long ago as 1127. The old fourteenth-century church with its Perpendicular tower seems to be subsiding and cracking up, while the neighbouring church of Adlingfleet in its untidy churchyard, partly grassed and partly paved with gravestones, seems in a hardly better state of repair. Both churches are sadly and surprisingly kept locked for fear of vandals, but one can see through the clear glass of Adlingfleet's east window on to its fourteenth- and sixteenth-century altar tombs and its box pews. Between the two churches, at an elbow in the road near where the Trent and Ouse join to form the Humber, is Ousefleet. Remote and peaceful, it was the most easterly point in the West Riding.

CHAPTER TWO

The Dales —
Harrogate and Craven

To the west of York are two more districts of North Yorkshire which were once (one wholly, the other partly) in the West Riding – Harrogate and Craven. Together they form what approximated most nearly in the Riding to a holiday area, although most of the visitors are weekenders. The region offers much to those interested in outdoor pursuits, and the Harrogate district is of particular interest to the historically minded. In a field near Boroughbridge are the Devil's Arrows – three large monoliths, each standing about 20 feet above the ground; no-one knows their real purpose, but they probably had some connection either with a New Stone Age or Bronze Age religious ritual or with prehistoric astronomy. At nearby Aldborough one can see a Roman pavement in the garden of the Aldborough Arm's Hotel, and an altar dedicated to Mercury in a parish church said to stand on the site of a Roman temple. Aldborough was, after the Roman invasion, the capital of the Brigantes, the biggest tribal group in Britain. Their queen, Cartimandua, collaborated with the Romans, to whom she betrayed Caractacus, perhaps in Aldborough itself where fragments of the city wall are still visible behind the excellent museum.

There is a complete towered Saxon church at Kirk Hammerton, although it is now only the south aisle of one built in the nineteenth century; and the district has around a score of those churches so common in the Vale of York which are either wholly or partially Norman. The oldest Christian building in the area is at Ripon: the 7th-century crypt of St Wilfred's monastery – all that is left of a church destroyed by the Danes in a 9th-century raid. Now part of a cathedral, in it is a narrow hole called St Wilfred's Needle, the ability to crawl through which from the crypt into the passage behind was regarded in medieval times as a proof of chastity.

The present cathedral chapter house may be all or part of the first of two Norman churches to be built on the site. Of the second only the north transept remains intact. The west front, which with its twin towers is perhaps the best known feature of the cathedral, was built by archbishop Walter de Grey in the thirteenth century when the Early English style was in vogue, but most of the lancet windows so characteristic of the period were put in by Sir George Gilbert Scott during the church's Victorian restoration.

Externally Ripon Minster has the look of austerity one associates with the North Country, but once inside the first thing the visitor notices is the colour. The choir screen has niches filled with brightly painted statues of people associated with the Church in Ripon over 1,200 years. They were given by friends of the cathedral in 1947 to replace those lost at the Reformation, the great upheaval in the Church which followed the break with the Pope in the reign of Henry VIII.

Perhaps the finest works of art in the cathedral are the fifteenth-century choir stalls made by members of Ripon's own school of carvers. The canons' seats have intricately carved, pinnacled canopies, and there are some marvellous bench ends. Instead of the usual poppy-head, one has an elephant with a castle on its back being defended by nine little men. There are fascinating carvings under the seats too. One shows Samson carrying off the gates of Gaza under his arm, and another a fox running away with a goose. Not all the carving is genuine medieval work; some of it is nineteenth-century restoration, but it is all splendid craftsmanship.

No famous men are buried here. St Wilfred's shrine once stood at the east end of the church and for centuries pilgrims came to it barefoot along Barefoot Street, but it was destroyed at the Reformation and the saint's bones were lost. There are one or two notable monuments though, including one to Hugh

Ripley, last wakeman and first mayor of Ripon, who died in 1637. The office of wakeman was Anglo-Saxon in origin. Elected by his fellow citizens the wakeman had to maintain law and order and to compensate anyone who was robbed. One of his duties was to set the watch by causing a horn to be blown, and the original Saxon horn still exists. Although the office of wakeman lapsed when the town got its borough charter in 1604, every night at nine o'clock a curious figure in black tricorn hat and fawn skirted tunic (and trousers !) emerges from the handsome classical town hall, crosses the road to the market cross and blows his horn to the four winds.

The 90-foot-high obelisk which serves as Ripon's market cross commemorates William Aislabie who erected it at his own expense in 1781 to commemorate his diamond jubilee as M.P. for the borough. Little wonder he was there 60 years; the right to vote depended on the ownership of certain houses called burgage tenements, and the Aislabies had inherited or bought up most of them. William's father, John, who himself sat for Ripon, was chancellor of the exchequer from 1717 to 1720, and he became involved in a scheme for getting rid of the National Debt by selling shares in a company with a monopoly of South Sea trade. Millions were invested but returns were nil and thousands were ruined. When investors realised the worthlessness of their shares and the South Sea Bubble burst, Aislabie was expelled from the Commons and retired to his estates at Studley Royal, a mile or two west of Ripon. The house there was destroyed by fire in 1946 and the Aislabies' successors, the Vyners, moved into the impressive stable block. John Aislabie occupied his forced retirement in laying out the grounds of his estate in the amazing style of the time, a project continued by later owners of the estate. The waters of the River Skell were used to make ornamental pools, a lake and a long, straight, lawn-flanked canal. From the east gate of the estate an avenue of trees was planted to provide a vista of the cathedral towers, while another, perhaps more famous, church building provides a Surprise View from near a cliff-top classical folly called the Temple of Fame. While other squires were having mock ruins built to give a picturesque appearance to their estates, the owners of Studley Royal went one better and bought probably the finest genuine monastic ruin in the country – Fountains Abbey. The abbey was founded in 1132 by some Benedictine monks from St Mary's Abbey, York, who, dissatisfied with the laxity of their monastery, adopted the more austere Cistercian rule. The Cistercians avoided the potential corruption of town life and lived in remote spots where they devoted themselves to the worship of God and to farming. In Yorkshire they specialized in sheep-rearing and thereby made their own contribution to the rise of the county's most characteristic industry. One of the most impressive ranges of buildings at Fountains includes a vast 300-foot-long cellar used at least in part for the storage of wool.

The early Cistercian monks tried to keep their monasteries as simple as possible, no matter how large they were. Excessive ornamentation was frowned upon and towers were particularly eschewed as symbols of pride. However, Abbot Marmaduke Huby, who presided at the abbey from 1494 till 1526, lived in laxer times than the house's founding fathers and could not resist the temptation to display his own and his house's pride by building a magnificent Perpendicular tower, today the most memorable feature of Fountains. But pride comes before a fall. The abbey was dissolved by Henry VIII's agents in 1539. In 1597 the site was purchased by a remarkable man called Stephen Proctor. His family had been yeoman tenants of the abbey in the Craven districts, but he made himself a fortune by dealing in leases of lead mines in Nidderdale, and set out to become a gentleman. He bought himself a knighthood from James I and a family tree showing fictitious connections with nobility from the College of Arms. Then with stones from the lay brothers' infirmary at the abbey he built a beautiful five-storey mansion, Fountains Hall. Yet despite all this, he was never accepted as an equal by the neighbouring gentry.

Fountains Hall is just one of several old houses in the Harrogate district which are open to the public. The oldest is fourteenth-century, moated Markenfield Hall, said to be the best surviving example in England of the manor house of a Plantagenet gentleman. A similar house at Spofforth, the repu-

8. Knaresborough and the River Nidd.

ted birthplace of Harry Hotspur, has long been a ruin, having been damaged by the Yorkists after its owner, the earl of Northumberland's death at Towton, and finally dismantled in 1604. Newby Hall at Skelton is a house of a different period – a red-brick mansion begun in 1705 for Sir Edward Blackett, whose family had made their fortune from coal mining in the north-east. It passed into the hands of William Weddell, who spent an inherited fortune on enlarging and enriching his house and acquiring pieces of antique sculpture. He had Robert Adam, the famous architect of Edinburgh New Town, build him a wing with three apartments specially designed to hold his collection.

Another largely eighteenth-century house is Ripley Castle. Only a small tower block remains of the original castle where Oliver Cromwell spent the night after the battle of Marston Moor. The family tradition is that the master of the house, Sir William Ingilby, was away at the time and his wife received the Parliamentary leader with a pair of pistols stuck in her belt. She watched him carefully through the night, and when he left in the morning told him that he would have paid for any ill-conduct with his life. The battle, in which the Fairfaxes also took part, was fought on a front extending approximately two miles from Tockwith to Long Marston. A clump of trees on rising ground just north of the York–Wetherby road (B.1224) marks the site of the Parliamentary headquarters. The Royalists were drawn up on the moor beyond a ditch which served as a natural trench and which can still be traced between the two villages. Marston Moor was a disaster for them. But the memorial obelisk on the battlefield was not put up to commemorate their dead; it is the Cromwellian Association's tribute to their hero's victory.

In happier days, Cromwell's enemy Charles I had stayed at Red House, the seat of the Slingsbys, in the next-door parish of Moor Monkton, and watched Sir Henry Slingsby's horse win a race on Acomb Moor. Red House is now a school but its chapel is a remarkable building which still retains complete its seventeenth-century fittings. Sir Henry's body was not buried here, however, but in Knaresborough parish church after he

9. The River Wharfe at Bolton Abbey.

had been beheaded on Tower Hill for Royalist activities during the Commonwealth period.

Knaresborough is one of the most photographed towns in England. Almost every book on Yorkshire contains a picture of the castellated railway bridge high above the River Nidd with the medieval church tower in the background. The river gorge has a well-deserved fame as a tourist resort, and a very pleasant Sunday afternoon can be spent rowing up and down stream, but the town has other attractions, not least its associations with Mother Shipton. Ursula Shipton is supposed to have been born in a cave in the cliffs above the river in 1488. She was famous as a prophetess even in her own day, the prophecy that brought her national fame being that Cardinal Wolsey, on his way north in 1530, would never be enthroned at York. In fact he got no further than Cawood. But the prophecies for which she is best known today – of the coming of the horseless carriage, the iron ship, the submarine and the wireless, and of the end of the world in 1881 (conveniently changed since to 1991) – were the nineteenth-century invention of one Charles Hindley of Brighton.

Close to Mother Shipton's cave is another famous Knaresborough phenomenon, the Dropping Well. Here, below a trickle of water running over a projecting block of limestone, are hung gloves, hats, eggs and other paraphernalia brought by visitors to be encrusted with the lime, sulphates, chlorides and magnesia contained in the water and within a period of four months to two years to acquire the appearance of being made of brown stone. But the waters of the Knaresborough district have other properties which have led that ancient town to be overshadowed and in a sense taken over by her upstart neighbour Harrogate, the administrative centre of a district which includes both Knaresborough and Ripon.

If one approaches Harrogate by train from the Leeds direction one's eye is caught by a domed and colonnaded rotunda on the left-hand side of the track, which, standing in a park which turns out to be the town's famous Stray, could at first sight be taken for a miniature bandstand or a mock classical temple. In fact it marks the site of the Tewit Well (tewit being the local name for the lapwing, a bird still found in the area), the foundation of Harrogate's fortunes. The spring was discovered in 1571 by William Slingsby of Bilton Hall while out riding in this part of Knaresborough Forest. He drank the water and the taste reminded him of the mineral waters he had drunk in the Belgian town of Spa. He had the area paved and walled and it became known as the English Spa, the first in the country. The Tewit Well in High Harrogate was a chalybeate spring, but soon others were discovered with a different content, including the sulphur springs half-a-mile away in Low Harrogate which according to a treatise written in 1626 by a Dr Deane 'cheereth and reviveth the spirit, strengtheneth the stomach, causeth good and quick appetite and furthereth digestion.'

Harrogate is built on the crest of a ridge or anticline pushed up by a volcanic upheaval not powerful enough to make an active crater. The lowest strata of the carboniferous series of rocks are exposed and through them springs percolate from a very great depth, that is from the underlying magma of igneous rock, and as they rise to the surface they bring with them the various minerals they meet on their way – strong sulphur, mild sulphur containing alkaline salts, saline chalybeate and pure chalybeate. Within an area of two miles there are 88 springs, and some of those which were commercially exploited can be identified from the little pump houses built over them, even though the functions of these buildings have changed. John's Well in High Harrogate is now a sweet shop; the Gothic Magnesia Well in the Valley Gardens is a gardener's hut; another little domed pump room in the gardens is an ice-cream kiosk; and the Montpellier well-house, close to the Crown Hotel, is a boutique. Not far away are the Royal Baths, opened in 1897 and the last to give the full spa treatment – massage-douche, berthe vapour, liver pack with needle or shower, and the Harrogate carbonic acid bath. Owing to the advance in medical knowledge, synthetic medicines and the improvement in the National Health Service, they ceased to give medical treatment in 1969, and although their building still houses a Turkish bath as well as a sauna, its chief attraction now is probably its restaurant where one can dine to the accompaniment of a 'palm court' orchestra. The bath chairs have gone and Harrogate today draws its biggest crowds for the annual Great Yorkshire Show, but it is still possible to 'take the waters', for they are the principal exhibit in the Royal Pump Room Museum. This is the handsome octagonal, domed building which was erected over the sulphur spring in 1842, when its former roof and colonnade were removed to cover the Tewit Well. It costs 4p to descend the steps from the main hall and drink as much as you wish of the water from what was known with justice as the 'stinking well'; it tastes like very salty rotten eggs!

At first sight Harrogate seems predominantly mid- to late Victorian and Edwardian in character, particularly if one arrives in the town by train. Although the tall station building itself was begun in 1964, its immediate vicinity could not be anything but Victorian. Here is the North Eastern Hotel, a statue of the Queen Empress under a canopy, Albert Street and Victoria Avenue, and, directly opposite the station entrance, verandahed shops, like those on Southport's Lord Street though much less well maintained. There are more of them down Parliament Street, the town's main shopping street, where one of the shops is a fantastic Gothic concoction with a hint of French Canada about it. But the *leit motif* of this part of Low Harrogate is the dome. The Royal Hall, once the 'Kursaal', which is used for conferences (for, with its abundance of accommodation, the old spa is now a notable trade exhibition and conference centre), is domed, and so are the Royal Baths. Across Crescent Gardens is a neo-Georgian town hall, but in the gardens the Victorian theme is played again in an iron bandstand, behind which is Farrah's Harrogate Toffee shop, established in 1840 and selling a confection which became almost as famous as the waters themselves. There are more domes, or rather half-domes, on the Crown Hotel, and then full ones on the Sun Pavilion in the Valley Gardens and on the former Grand Hotel in Cornwall Road, which like some other hotels in the town has had to change its rôle. The Grand is in the process of becoming Windsor House prestige offices, and the Harlow Manor Hydro with its Gothic spire was taken over by the Ministry of Works, and parts have been let off as offices to other bodies. The Prince of Wales of the 1860s is now Prince of Wales Mansions. The hotels of Harrogate would make a marvellous subject for a Ph.D. thesis. The most striking is the huge Hotel Majestic, domed again and of red brick, looking among the blackened Yorkshire stone like a refugee from Blackpool's North Prom., or an oversized reject from Llandrindod Wells. It was built in 1900.

It is not surprising perhaps that the area of the Valley Gardens with the natural magnet of 36 springs, each of a different chemical composition, should reflect the opulence of the days when the British Empire was at its zenith. But there is another Harrogate half-a-mile away, a pleasant survival from an earlier, less showy age. This is High Harrogate, the first part to develop but left behind once the duchy of Lancaster began to encourage building on its estate in Low Harrogate in the 1840s. The region of John's Well with its bow windows and fanlights is redolent of the days of Jane Austen, although some of the late Georgian-style houses fronting the marvellous green sward of the Stray may have been built after her time.

The most interesting buildings in this area are probably the hotels. At one of them, the Granby Hall, in the days when it was the Royal Oak, that remarkable character Blind Jack of Knaresborough, blinded by smallpox at six and yet one of the most notable road builders of all time, used to earn himself a few copper playing the fiddle before he embarked on his eminently successful career. The hotel has been enlarged considerably since his time, but its neighbour the pleasant, colourwashed County Hotel probably looks much as it did some 200 years ago. Another High Harrogate inn, the Dragon, had as its landlord the father of William Powell Frith, famous as the painter of Victorian crowd scenes like *Derby Day* and *The Railway Station*. There is a minor work of his in Harrogate's art gallery. A charming period piece called *Many Happy Returns of the Day*, it shows three or four generations of a family sitting round a heavily laden table, the most conspicuous item on it an iced cake inscribed 'Alice'. Alice herself presides from a garlanded chair, while the rest of the children knock back the claret.

There is a memorial tablet to Frith in Christ Church, the parish church of High Harrogate, which appears isolated on a triangular island of the Stray called Church Square, between Park Parade, Skipton Road and Knaresborough Road. It was built in 1831, but the site of its predecessor can be identified just to the north where two paths cross the square and meet at nothing more than the churchyard wall. In the vestry is a print of the church before the transepts were added in 1862 and another copy of the same print with the transepts etched in. Nearby hang photographs of past vicars and curates, a number of whom (the curates more often than the vicars), as so often happens after a start in a fashionable church like this, rose to high office. As though to encourage his successors, the pastoral staff of a former vicar, P. F. D. de Labbilière, who became bishop suffragan of Knaresborough and dean of Westminster, is kept in a glass case in a side chapel.

Harrogate is rich in affluent looking churches designed by famous architects and enriched by the well-to-do who came here to take the waters or to retire. Perhaps the most pleasing externally is Sir Walter Tapper's St Mary's. Built in 1916 to a cruciform plan with a square central tower, its white stone has weathered and, although in suburbia, it has the appearance of an ancient country church. The most dramatic is St Wilfred's, the masterpiece of Temple Moore, and it has an amazing neighbour, the huge, partially timbered Harrogate College which looks as if it belongs to Bournemouth or Woodhall Spa rather than to Yorkshire. The church is built of clean smooth stone, but all round the inside walls are colourful scenes from the life of Christ, the characters in them with the faces of people who once belonged to St Wilfred's congregation. An ambulatory round the chancel leads to the Lady Chapel. The architect believed in surprises, and here is one, though it was created after his death – a dramatic view back over the high altar, up on a higher level than the chapel, of two crosses, altar and rood, and of stone vaulting beyond. The atmosphere is very cathedral-like. St Wilfred's was largely the gift of a woman who only came to live in Harrogate by accident. Her sister, to whom the west window is a memorial, died in the town while breaking a journey to Scotland.

St Wilfred's may be the best church in Harrogate in the architectural sense but it is not the best known to visitors. That distinction must go to St Peter's, the big black church with the patterned slate roof which stands by the war memorial obelisk right in the centre of town, with Parliament Street to its left and West Park to its right. Although only finished in 1926 when its tower was put up, it looks older and in keeping with its neighbour, the mid-Victorian Prospect Hotel. Inside the most noticeable feature, in fact an immediate shock on entering, are the huge mitred heads and shoulders of bishops in roundels above each of the pillars in the nave, but unfortunately there is no record of whom they represent. The whole interior is impressive, particularly the French-looking apsidal east end with its gilded reredos, but regrettably St Peter's is threatened with closure in this age when the Church appears to have lost its sense of mission.

St Peter's overlooks the town end of the Stray, which must be the feature of Harrogate the visitor will remember when he has forgotten all else but the Pump Room water. This park-like common of 215 acres was first acquired for the use of the townspeople when Knaresborough Forest was enclosed for agricultural purposes by Act of Parliament in 1770. The intention was to protect the springs and ensure public access to them. For a long time the Stray was used for grazing, but in 1893 the corporation purchased the grazing rights and gradually coverted it into the acres of well-kept lawn we see today.

Harrogate has other scenic delights, particularly Harlow Car Gardens, the trial gardens of the Northern Horticultural Society, where almost every aspect of gardening is represented. Among the specialist gardens are the heath garden, the sandstone garden, the peat beds, the rose garden and the foliage garden, the last devoted entirely to plants suitable for flower arrangement. It is a beautiful place, but the district is full of beautiful sights and some of them are unforgettable. One of these is the view across the River Ure to the old North Riding village of West Tanfield, all yellow limestone walls and red pantile roofs which, with the gateway tower of the castle of the Marmions and the Perpendicular tower of the church, create a unique village skyline.

Another breathtaking view is that of Nidderdale from high up by Middlesmoor church. The dale is a popular haunt of weekend motorists who buy their families tea in Pateley Bridge and take them to see the waterfall at Wath, Stump Cross Caverns, or the amazing Brimham Rocks which were eroded into fantastic shapes by sandstorms in the far-off Permian Age when Britain was a desert. With all their attractions in terms of beauty spots and curiosities it is easily forgotten that Nidderdale and neighbouring Washburndale were once a highly industrialised part of the West Riding. It was principally a linen manufacturing area, since, when the textile industry was mechanized, it was at a disadvantage where wool was concerned in being a long way from the nearest woollen cloth marketing centre at Leeds. But a large number of the mills which at one time produced linen yarn and cloth have closed down. Some of them closed as long ago as the 1830s. One of the problems was the difficulty of obtaining cheap coal, which meant that many of the mills which did survive the slumps of the 'thirties and 'forties continued to be water-powered when elsewhere in the Riding the steam engine was being increasingly employed. Other problems were increased mechanization in Ulster and the competition of cheap cotton, some of which was also manufactured in Nidderdale. Nor was the local supply of flax by any means sufficient. In the 1850s when Britain was at war with Russia, her main source of flax, further mills closed, and more went when the increased use of the sewing machine made cotton thread preferable because of its elasticity and when increased tariffs in the U.S.A. blocked the main foreign outlet for linen thread. And as cotton cloth improved too the linen market got smaller. Some mills were converted to other manufactures, such as silk (which did not last long), twine, cords and rope, although rope and twine making was concentrated in quite a small area of Nidderdale between Foster Beck and Fringill. In recent years this industry, which began to contract between the wars, has been hard-hit by the increase in the use of artificial fibres, something of course which has also affected the cotton industry, and, although it carries on the local textile tradition, it is somewhat ironic that the I.C.I. fibres division headquarters is in Harrogate. A few mills still operate and linen is still produced on a small scale, as is rope, but one mill is now a restaurant (the Knox Manor at Low Laithe), while others are ruins, a happy hunting ground for the industrial archaeologist, who can still identify wheelhouses and watercourses and occasionally may come across a waterwheel like that at Foster Beck which was installed as recently as 1904 and damage to which caused the closure of the mill in 1966.

Also of interest to the industrial archaeologist are the relics of mining in the area. Lead mining has been carried on here in the limestone country west of Pateley Bridge since at least Roman times. Two pigs of lead bearing the names of the emperors Trajan and Domitian were found at Dacre at the side of a track leading to Aldborough. Monks were exploiting the lead and iron deposits in the area in the twelfth century and about 1446 Fountains Abbey erected a smelt mill at the hamlet which came to be known as Smelthouses, near Pateley Bridge. The main developments in mining in the area took place in the nineteenth century, after the passing of the Limited Liability Company Act, when miners were drawn to the Dales from Wales, Scotland, Ireland, Derbyshire and Cornwall. But due to a combination of increasing cheap foreign competition, which eventually led Dales miners to seek work in Spain, a shortage of working capital and several slumps in the price of lead, the mines were, but for a few isolated examples, closed down by 1896. A revival started in 1914, stimulated by the demands of the Great War, but when the war was over, a decline set in again, and since then no large-scale mining has been attempted. It is possible to trace the veins of ore by looking out for spoil dumps, some of which have been exploited in recent years as a source of barytes, used for white paint, and fluorspar, natural calcium fluoride. It is possible too to discover entrances to shafts or adits, driven horizontally into the hillsides over a period of more than a thousand years. The two oldest on Greenhow Hill, on the Pateley Bridge-Grassington road (B.6265), where the miners' cottages are now occupied by weekenders from the cities, the Jack Ass and Sam Oon levels, known to miners as the work of 'T'owd man', are believed to be of Roman or medieval origin. Not far away are the remains of the Cockhill smelt mill and the dressing floor where the ore was separated from the waste before smelting, while at Merryfield Hole is the ruined engine house of a vertical shaft mine. But Nidderdale is only on the fringe of a considerable lead-mining area which extends well over the district boundary into Craven and the Yorkshire Dales National Park.

The name Craven is probably British in origin. Although some scholars claim that it is derived from *craf*, meaning garlic, a more plausible explanation is that it was originally *craig faen*, meaning the stony rock, translated later into the name of the local wapentake, Staincliffe. The stone is predominantly lime-stone, exposed in a great fault which runs east-west from Pateley Bridge to Ingleton. Like Nidderdale, the district is not usually thought of as an industrial area, but industry there was and to some extent still is. In Lothersdale, where Charlotte Brontë was a governess at a house called Stonne Gappe, the Gateshead of her *Jane Eyre,* there is a silk mill which is still working and which retains its waterwheel. And Skipton – sheep town – Craven's capital, has an industrial side to its character. It is well-named, for sheep sales in its market have been known to exceed £120,000 in a single day, but the largest firm in the town, although once manufacturing worsted cloth, now produces Terylene and other threads for the tailoring and dressmaking trades. This side of Skipton's activities is overlooked by the visitor, just as are the Victorian working class housing areas of Newtown and Middletown, and off the Broughton and Gargrave roads.

The mecca of the day-tripper is the broad High Street, the market place of Skipton, at the top of which is the great castle of the Cliffords, the family of the 'Butcher'. As it stands today the castle dates largely from the time of the last of the Cliffords, Anne, countess of Pembroke, who rebuilt it after it had been damaged by the Parliamentary army in the Civil War. She also rebuilt the tower of the church next door and completed the almhouses for indigent ladies founded in 1593 by her mother the countess of Cumberland at Beamsley in Wharfedale. There are some more imposing almshouses in Linton, another Wharfedale village. Founded in 1721, with a dome-towered chapel in the centre they have been described as looking like a miniature town hall. They front a green with a maypole and a very odd sundial won by Linton in 1949 in a competition to find the prettiest village in the North.

Wharfedale is said to be the most beautiful of the Dales. It is certainly the most frequented by the weekend visitors and tourists. They play cricket on the grass near Bolton Abbey, which is in reality not an abbey at all but the partly ruined church of an Augustinian priory, and they cross the river Wharfe there by its 57 stepping stones, while the more foolhardy among them try to jump or even stride across the Strid, a narrow chasm, four to five feet across and from sixty to eighty feet long, through which the Wharfe, which only a few yards upstream is 50 feet wide, rushes with great rapidity.

A mile or two above the Strid is the Cliffords' hunting lodge, Barden Tower, and the handsome seventeenth-century Barden Bridge, and, a little way above that, Appletreewick, where the village street tumbles downhill past old houses like the stepped- and pigeon-holed Monk's Hall, once a grange (or sheep farm) of Bolton Abbey. Appletreewick was the birth-place of Yorkshire's Dick Whittington – Sir William Craven. He was born in 1548 in one of the two cottages which now form the church of St John, and at 13 or 14 was sent to London by common carrier and bound apprentice to one Robert Hudson, citizen and merchant tailor. In time William became a master craftsman and eventually was elected lord mayor of London, but he never forgot his fellow Yorkshiremen back in Wharfedale. He restored his parish church at Burnsall, rebuilt Burnsall bridge and endowed the grammar school.

Burnsall is one of the most popular tourist spots in the dale. The car park by the river is nearly always full in the summer months, and every day, bar Sunday, men fish from the village green while their children eat ice cream, and their wives and girl-friends wander about the cool interior of the church, gaping at the Norse hog-back tombstones (one with two well-preserved monster heads and a scaly back), and try to decipher the sixteenth-century registers. Perhaps even more popular is Grassington, the generally acknowledged capital of Upper Wharfedale. The pleasant cobbled square of this grey old mining village (a popular setting for television plays) is usually covered with motor cars, and a new coach park has been opened at the top of the main street with a children's playground as its neighbour. The visitors bring lots of trade into town, but are not always welcome. Residents have had to put up *Keep Out* notices to prevent them from wandering up their garden paths to admire the view. A little way up the dale at Kilnsey a notice warns against the dangers of climbing Kilnsey Crag, whose sphinx-like shape is the product partly of the Craven fault and partly of erosion caused by a glacier which filled the dale in the last Ice Age.

Above Kilnsey is Kettlewell, an attractive village below the brooding mass of 2,310-foot-high Great Whernside. One of the roads out of Kettlewell goes over Park Rash to Coverdale. If you can put up with cattle grids, opening and closing gates, and steep 'S' bends, this lane, once part of the London to Richmond coaching route, with its wide views over into Wensleydale, provides one of the most exhilarating motor runs in the country. The main road continues to Starbotton, a village dating largely from the seventeenth century, for a disastrous flood in June 1686 swept most of the old village away and people from all over the country contributed to the relief of the distressed. Beyond Starbotton is Buckden, once the home of the foresters of Langstrothdale Chase, with the Buck Inn, a relatively unspoilt Georgian coaching inn in a most attractive setting. From here the main road continues through the Kidstones Pass into Bishopdale, while another branches off for Langstrothdale and the village of Hubberholme. Hubberholme church is built in a style peculiar to the area around Craven – long and low, as though squatting to protect itself from the elements, with nave, chancel and aisles all under one roof.

St Michael's, Hubberholme is a chapel of ease to St Oswald's at Arncliffe, which lies over the fell in Littondale, a tributary valley to Wharfedale, south-west of Langstrothdale. South of Arncliffe are the foundations of Iron Age huts set among ancient Celtic fields, square or rectangular in shape, whose presence is betrayed by lynchets – stepped terraces on the hillsides to allow level ploughing. Later Anglian lynchets can be identified around Malham, but the characteristic field marker of the area is the dry-stone wall. Dry-stone walls are an unforgettable feature of the Dales, there are so many of them. Above the Craven fault they are of bright, light grey limestone; below it they are of a darker but clean gritstone, and further south they become darker still, blackened by the smoke of industry. The character of the houses changes with that of the walls. In the limestone country they are built of random or rubble walling bound at the corners by quoins made of good sandstone or carefully dressed limestone, with sandstone door and window frames, but further south they are generally built entirely of smooth coal measures sandstone or gritstone blocks.

The field walls around any Dales village can be of many different dates and deserve careful study. In the parts settled by Anglian, as opposed to Norse, immigrants, the land was farmed in medieval times by the open field system. Large fields were shared out among the villagers who had widely scattered strips in an attempt to guarantee a fair share of good and poor land. In Conistone township, across the Wharfe from Kilnsey, all the farms (which have their own immediate walls) are together in the village, from which the open fields, North Field and South Field, were once worked. Such village fields were surrounded by walls way back in the Middle Ages. These walls can often be identified, although they may be irregular in line because heavy boulders were often used as a foundation and it was easier to move the line of a wall than the boulders. In time extensions were sometimes made to a village's fields and, as for example at Linton, there may be other ancient walls beyond the first set. But for various practical reasons, by exchange and sale, strips were eventually amalgamated to form compact fields and so we have walls within walls. The older subsidiary enclosures of perhaps 400 years ago are walled in a reversed 'S' pattern, representing the sweep of the medieval plough as it was turned round. In the eighteenth century, enclosure of remaining open field was made on a regular pattern by Parliamentary commissioners and thus fields of this time are usually square or oblong in shape. Meanwhile walls had been constructed up the hillsides beyond the boundaries of the old open fields to take in common land and pasture. It was felt that the pastures would be improved by enclosure and by the regulation or 'stinting' of the number of animals using them. And so the present pattern of walls was established and the hand of man now seems to lie heavy on the Dales.

It is not because of its dry-stone walls or even its Celtic fields that Littondale is well-known to thousands who have never been to Yorkshire, but because it was the setting of the popular television series *Emmerdale Farm*, and the Falcon Inn at Arncliffe is familiar as Amos Brearley's 'Woolpack'. (The farm itself is at Leathley near Otley.) Long before the television age, Littondale was used by Charles Kingsley to set another story, *The Water Babies*; he called it Vendale. Miss Elizabeth Hammond, who lived at Bridge End House, Arncliffe, is said to have been the original of the 'woman in the red petticoat' who took care of Tom the chimney sweep after his exhausting walk from Hartover Place, where he had slipped, a sooty intruder, into little Ellie's gorgeous bedroom and had been chased away by the whole household. At the bottom of Bridge End's garden is the River Skirfare into which Tom slipped to become a water baby.

The original Hartover Place is Malham Tarn House (now a field studies centre), where Kingsley was staying as the guest of the Morrison family when he wrote his book. Malham Tarn is not only the largest natural lake in the Riding, it is also a most surprising feature in this area of porous limestone rock. It survives because it lies on a bed of harder rock, Silurian slate, which is impervious to water and recurs in patches along the line of the Craven fault. Perhaps the most impressive feature of Malhamdale, the upper part of Airedale, is Malham Cove, below the lake, a great limestone amphitheatre, with walls 300 feet high, which is part of the fault. It is so tough a climb to the top that it is being used at the time of writing as a practice ground by members of the joint British Army/Royal Nepalese Army Everest Expedition.

Among the other natural phenomena of the limestone country are the caves and potholes created by water seeping through the porous stone. Gordale Scar, close to Malham Cove, which has been painted by a number of famous artists including John Piper, is a cave whose roof has collapsed. Off the road between Malham and the pleasant little town of Settle, in the face of Langcliffe Scar, is the Victoria Cave, discovered by a dog on Coronation Day 1838. Rich in animal and human remains, 20,000 years ago, when Britain had a tropical climate, it was probably a hyena's den. Later it may have housed the cave bear and was possibly a refuge for Romans from a camp at Ilkley at the time of a British insurrection.

Further west, on the Kendal road (A.65), is the village of Clapham where almost every cottage garden contains descendants of plants brought back from his travels in the East by Reginald Farrer, whose rock garden in the grounds of Ingleborough Hall was once world famous. There is a pleasant walk through these grounds to Ingleborough cave, where there are some amazing stalactites and stalagmites with names like the Jockey's Cap, the Maiden's Couch, Elephant Legs and the Ring o' Bells. From the cave there is a path up Trow Gill, a deep shadowy limestone valley where the sheep are almost camouflaged amongst the stones, to the narrow entrance to Gaping Ghyl, a 340-foot-deep pothole, which can be descended with the aid of a winch in 90 seconds, leading to caves the size of cathedrals. From Gaping Ghyl the path continues to the summit of Ingleborough, where prehistoric man had a stronghold on the plateau 2,373 feet up. South-west of the hill, in the valley of the Greta, is the village of Ingleton, the start of what is called the Falls Walk, a circular trip up the valley of the Doe or Dale Beck and back down the Twiss valley, with waterfalls of all shapes and sizes breaking over the oldest rocks in Yorkshire, pre-Cambrian in age, notably the beautiful 46-foot-high Thornton Force. For the more energetic there is the Three Peaks Walk over Ingleborough, Whernside and Pen-y-ghent, hills all over 2,000 feet, which shut in the Ribble valley on three sides. A good centre to start the walk from is Horton-in-Ribblesdale, an often rain-and-wind-swept spot in what is probably the wildest of the Dales, with a grey old church whose Norman pillars all lean crazily towards the south. The little café here is thronged at weekends with young men, many of them from miles away in what was South Lancashire, who come for the potholing. Pen-y-ghent and Horton Moor are riddled with holes – Gable Rigg Pot, Churn Milk Hole, Hunt Pot, Hull Pot, Jackdaw Hole.

There is so much to be enjoyed in these wide open spaces with their good clean air. In Spring the bubble of the curlew is carried along to you on the breeze that caresses the gritstone tops of Yorkshire's tall mountains, while the acrobatic peewit loops about above the long grass on the slopes. In high summer the ring ousel, a white breasted mountain blackbird known locally as the heath throstle, sounds its alarm note *tac-tac-tac* in response to the advance of walkers or a sudden blast from the quarries on the side of Ingleborough, and eternally startled rabbits dart through grass tinged with tender bird's eye pink. What a tonic it is to come up here from office or mill or mine and forget the problems and stresses of working life. But beware the rain! The average annual rainfall at Ribblehead is 78.7 inches (it was 109.5 in 1954), compared with 38.6 at Halifax, which is bad enough.

It must have been a tough life in more ways than one for the navvies who came up to this remote part of Yorkshire back in the 1870s to build the amazing Settle-to-Carlisle railway line, (take a trip on it while it is still open), at the then phenomenal cost of £47,500 a mile. Many of these men, who lived in shanty towns with names like Jericho, Salt Lake City and Sebastopol lost their lives on the job, cutting their way through boulder-clay (the terminal moraine of a glacier), gritstone and black marble, and over a hundred of them are buried in the church-yard at Chapel-le-Dale, not far from their great 165-foot-high

10. & 11.   *above: left* 18th century carving over a cottage, Heptonstall; *right* Carving on font, Aston church. 12. *below* detail of 17th century monument to Shireburne family, Great Mitton.

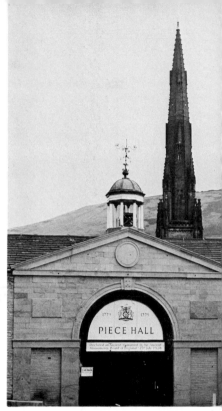

viaduct and embankment where the line is around 1,000 feet above sea level and about to pass out of Ribblesdale into the valley of the Dee, and from North Yorkshire into Cumbria.

13. & 14. *above: left* Cartwright Hall, Bradford's museum on the site of Samuel Cunliffe Lister's house at Manningham; *right* The Halifax Piece Hall and Square Congregational church, with Beacon Hill in the background. 15. *below* Skipton Castle: the gateway restored by Lady Anne Clifford.

CHAPTER THREE

West of the Pennines — Sedbergh, Bowland and Saddleworth

The former rural district of Sedbergh is not only no longer in the West Riding but no longer has a Yorkshire address. Although it remains within the boundaries of the Yorkshire Dales National Park, it is now part of the South Lakeland District of the new county of Cumbria and is administered from Kendal. But one imagines that the people of the area will long continue to think of themselves as Yorkshire folk, and even when they do not there will always be something there to remind them of their West Riding past – like, for instance, the inscription on a little bridge over Cowgill beck in the dale of Dent:

This bridg. repered at the charg. of the West Riding A.D. 1702.

It was, however, a logical move of the boundary commissioners to chop off this north-western corner of the county in their policy of rationalization. In most respects it is a westward-looking area – its three rivers flow west to join the Lune on its journey to the Irish Sea, and Kendal, a mere ten miles from Sedbergh by the A.684, is naturally the local shopping centre, any West Riding town of comparable size being many miles further away. And there is no major road, not even one with a B classification, to link the area with the rest of the Riding.

There has always been an air of remoteness and of being different from the rest of the county about these 52,500 acres of the parishes of Sedbergh, Dent and Garsdale formerly bounded on two sides by Westmorland and on another by the

74

North Riding. The physical appearance of the landscape is itself 'different'. The fells to the north and west of the district are not of lime or gritstone but of slaty rocks related to those of the Lake District. The sides of these domed hills are pale green in colour and large stretches, particularly on Howgill Fells, are unbroken by walls and fences, having been common grazing land for many centuries, a fact which explains their velvety smooth appearance. It is essentially an area of isolated farms scattered along the lower slopes rather than of valley bottom villages, a reflection of the settlement pattern of the Norse immigrants of a thousand years ago. Most of the farms have a *laithe,* a combined cowshed and barn for the hay on which half-a-dozen dairy cattle are fed during the winter. The far more numerous sheep spend most of their time out-of-doors. The laithes and farm houses, often both under one roof, are generally built from a yellowy-brown sandstone from the local Yoredale series of rocks which breaks easily into rectangular blocks. Lintels, doorheads and floors are made from locally quarried flags. Some of the houses have stone-framed windows and sometimes mullions, but the thinness of the flags makes them unsuitable for spanning a wide opening, so that the windows in this area tend to be noticeably smaller than elsewhere. Another noticeable feature of these houses is the round Westmorland-type chimney stack, often on a massive square base which either comes up from ground level as a projection on the gable or is carried out on corbels built out from the gable at about the level of the eaves. There are particularly fine examples of these chimneys at Gibbs Hall, Biggerside and High Hall in Dent. Many of the houses of the yeoman farmers, or statesmen as they were called locally, date from the seventeenth century when they replaced wood and plaster buildings supported by crucks – curved branches or trunks of trees split lengthways and then leant against each other to form an arch and joined by a crosspiece about six feet from the ground. But even in the cruck houses, gable ends had sometimes been built of stone and these were occasionally incorporated into the newer all-stone buildings, as for example at Low House, Garsdale. A complete cruck house, formerly thatched, survives at

The Hill in Sedbergh. Also in Sedbergh is Webster's shop, a timber building of the first half of the seventeenth century with a gabled front and large built-out chimney. It was once the town house of the Otways, one of whom, Sir John Otway, played a prominent part in Charles II's restoration. Not far from Webster's in Sedbergh's Main Street is the Golden Lion which has *in situ* what was a common feature of the seventeenth-century houses of the district, a Jacobean court cupboard built into a panelled screen.

Although the population of the whole district is only 3,250, Sedbergh, the largest settlement, has a town-like appearance, particularly in the narrow main street which is closed in by tall buildings, especially hotels, that seem to be conspiring to protect the shoppers from the wilderness and wet which lie at their backdoors. And indeed it is a market town, with a produce market on Wednesdays and a cattle market on Fridays, but as in the East Midland towns of Oundle and Uppingham, a good half of the place seems to be school buildings, although here they do not encroach on the actual town centre to quite the same degree.

Sedbergh School was founded around the year 1525 by Roger Lupton, a native of Howgill who became provost of Eton. Among its several very famous teachers was self-taught John Dawson of Garsdale, who coached eleven Senior Wranglers (top mathematics graduates at Cambridge). He died in 1820 and is commemorated by a bust on the south wall of the nave of Sedbergh church. There is a different kind of memorial to one of Dawson's pupils, Adam Sedgwick. He was a most distinguished professor of geology at Cambridge, although he had never studied the subject until he was elected to the chair in 1818, and he is remembered in his home town of Dent by a fountain made from a single block of granite inscribed with his name and the years of his birth and death.

Sedgwick's birthplace is generally known as Dent Town, while the dale it is in, the valley of the River Dee, is simply Dent. But it is more of a village than a town, although as long ago as 1429 it had its own local council of 24 statesmen who still choose the vicar. It was for a long time an important textile

76

centre, noted particularly for the knitting of worsted stockings. The men, women and children all knitted all day long, and poet laureate Robert Southey nicknamed them the 'terrible knitters of Dent'. In 1801 the average weekly production of the Sedbergh and Dent stocking knitters was 840 pairs; today the textile industry is represented in the area by a single woollen mill. The knitting was done at home in first-floor galleries open to the air, and neighbours were able to have a good chat if they could be heard over the sound of the needles. The galleries were removed from Dent Town's main street because they were an obstacle to traffic, which has always found the narrow cobbled thoroughfare difficult to negotiate. But one gallery has been reconstructed there, and an original survives in Railton Yard, Sedbergh.

Perhaps the most interesting building in the whole area is at Brigflatts, in what was a hamlet of flax weavers. Here the Quaker leader George Fox was once greeted by a crowd of 500, and here still stands the Friends' Meeting House of 1675 with its original fittings, including a dog-pen at the foot of the gallery stairs.

But as over the hill at Ribblehead, it is the railway that is the most impressive man-made feature in the landscape. Here are more striking landmarks, like, for example, Arten Gill viaduct, near the site of the navvies' shanty town of Ten Huts, and here too another reminder that in its building the railway took a heavy toll of life. The yard of Cowgill church was enlarged to accommodate its victims, who were laid in unmarked graves behind the church. And while Ribblehead viaduct is the highest in Yorkshire, Dent's station was the highest main line station in England – 'was' because it is now closed most of the time. A traveller arriving at the station used to be greeted by palisades of upended sleepers erected to check snowdrifts which have been known to block the line for long periods – a warning rather than a welcome to the visitor to this remotest corner of the West Riding.

While much of the Dales National Park, and particularly Wharfedale, criss-crossed by miles of dry-stone walling, seems, for all its loveliness, a landscape controlled and partially created by man, the ancient royal forest of Bowland, an area of outstanding natural beauty, appears at first sight untamed and unspoilt, a naturalist's paradise. Here on the limestone moorland slopes grow rare wild orchids – green frog, white great butterfly and pink fragrant – and the rare sika stag grazes the open moor around Stephen Park, haunt of the short-eared owl. But the deer, dark coated in winter and spotted red in summer, originated from crossbred Japanese-Formosan stock only introduced into Wyresdale and Gisburn Parks at the beginning of this century. Indeed much of Bowland's beauty is, despite first appearances, a product of man's intervention in the countryside. 3,000-acre Gisburn Forest, a woodland of Japanese larch, sitka, Scots and Formby pine, and lodge pole is barely 50 years old. In it are 200 nesting boxes which attract tits, kestrels and barn owls. The area is rich in bird life, largely because man has interfered with nature. The 344-acre Stocks Reservoir, itself fringed by plantations, is the haunt of migrating winter goosanders which fish its waters for trout, and sometimes they are joined by whistling flocks of up to 300 wigeon, as well as mallard, golden eye, pochard, tufted duck, scoter and shelduck. And since 1955 the reservoir has been the breeding ground of the red-breasted merganser. Under its waters lies the old village of Stocks-in-Bolland – 20 cottages, a shop, a post office, and a public house. There was a church too; consecrated in 1852, it was demolished in 1925, and its stones were used to build the present little church of St James. The cost was borne by the Fylde Water Board, for the reservoir was constructed to supply water to that area of Lancashire. Now Bowland – its name means 'land of cattle' – is itself in Lancashire, part of its Ribble Valley district.

The Trough of Bowland, a small and attractive ravine carved by melt-water from glaciers, where heather and bracken lap against the road, has long been popular with weekend and bank holiday motorists. There are village hall teas, and ice cream vans park on the verges to cater for the occupants of the hundreds of cars which journey nose-to-tail along this old main, but now unclassified road from Clitheroe to Lancaster, up which the Lancashire witches passed on their way to their trial at Lancaster Castle three and half centuries ago. But much of Bowland has escaped the attentions of the lolly licker and the litter dropper. The main villages are tucked away so unobtrusively in the Hodder valley that they add to the illusion that man has done his best to leave this wild and beautiful countryside to nature's care. Slaidburn, perhaps Bowland's equivalent of Dartmoor's Widecombe, has a fine church with exceptionally fine fittings – an Elizabethan font cover, a Jacobean screen and box pews. With its dog whips, a communion table instead of an altar, and a handsome three-decker pulpit still put to its old use – prayers said from the bottom deck, lessons read from the middle and sermons preached from the top – entering the church would be like stepping back into the eighteenth century were it not for the large Victorian east window of the Adoration of the Magi. Slaidburn is the former forest capital. The descendants of the hereditary keepers (or parkers) of the forest are the Parkers of Browsholme Hall, their home since the fourteenth century. The present house dates from 1507 and was given its red sandstone front in 1604.

Near where the Hodder, the former boundary between Lancashire and Yorkshire, flows into the Ribble is the thirteenth-century church of Great Mitton. Its north chapel has a splendid display of monuments to another ancient family, the Shireburnes, who lived across the county boundary in what is now the famous Jesuit school, Stonyhurst.

Mitton is one of several lovely villages on the fringe of Bowland. Perhaps the most attractive of all is Bolton, with market cross and stocks on one of its two village greens and lots of pretty whitewashed cottages. In the now demolished Bolton Hall, Sir Ralph Pudsey sheltered the fugitive Henry VI from the Yorkists after the battle of Hexham in 1464, and the king is reputed to have designed Bolton's very fine church tower. Near the site of the Hall is the roofed and walled King Henry's Well. There are two traditions connected with it: one that it was constructed as a bath for the King and the other that the monarch was a water-diviner and actually discovered the spring himself. From Bolton he visited both Bracewell, where he may have been entertained by the Tempest family in a house south-west of the church known as King Henry's Parlour, and also another of the Tempests' houses, Waddington Old Hall. It was here that he was captured, apparently after being betrayed by a monk, and, after a year of concealment, sent to London with his legs tied to the stirrups of his horse and with his face towards its tail.

The monks of Lancashire's Whalley Abbey, the home of King Henry's betrayer, were to resist Dissolution in the Pilgrimage of Grace, as were those of its West Riding neighbour Sawley, whose last abbot was hanged for his part in the rebellion. The remains of this Cistercian monastery founded in 1147 can be seen to the north of the main A.59 road between Skipton and Clitheroe. Actually, when compared with other Yorkshire abbeys, there is not a great deal left *in situ* (for Sawley was built of a poor material – calcareous shale) and admission is free. But the foundations of the buildings have been excavated and there are some interesting tombstones. In the south transept is the tomb slab of William of Rimington, prior of Sawley and chancellor of Oxford university, an opponent of the fourteenth-century reformer John Wycliffe. He took his name from the little village of Rimington, just a couple of miles from Sawley. In the nineteenth century it was to have a tune named after it, that of the well-known hymn, *Jesus shall reign*. Its first line is carved on the gravestone of its composer, Francis Duckworth, in Gisburn churchyard.

Gisburn has long been regarded as the gateway to Yorkshire from the west and is well known to the Lancashire holidaymaker heading for the Dales and the east coast for the shops and cafés along its main and virtually only street, and for its splendid old pubs. South of the village is the former urban district of Barnoldswick. Despite the white roses on its coat of arms, Barnoldswick has also been shunted across the border into Lancashire, to be part of its Pendle District. Mind you, although diversification followed the slump of the 1930s and Rolls Royce moved in as well as firms making plastics and filters for the brewing trade, it is a cotton town and its men have always followed the fortunes of Lancashire's Burnley football club. There has been quite a lot of migration from the other side of the border too, but the people of Barnoldswick (the Barlickers) have always regarded themselves as almost a race apart. The original settlement was Anglian, the *wick* or farm of Bernulf the thane. After the Conquest the land passed into the hands of the de Lacys who had a castle at nearby Clitheroe, though their main seat was at Pontefract. Henry de Lacy tried to settle some Cistercian monks here, but they did not like the climate (their grain rotted in the field) or the people, who complained when the monks replaced the village church with one of their own, and after a stay of six years, they moved to a fresh site by the Aire at Kirkstall. Barnoldswick became a grange of Kirkstall, and the monks' church, tucked out of the way, as Cistercian churches so often are, in the Gill a mile from the village, remained the parish church. St Mary-le-Gill is still there in its little valley among the yew trees, though it is not the original building put up by the monks.

Another manufacturing town with ancient roots is Barnoldswick's neighbour Earby. Its most interesting old building is its mullion-windowed grammar school of 1658 which is now a clinic. The church, begun in 1909, was never finished and lacks a north aisle and tower. Seen from the moors to the east, this little cotton town and its magnificent Pennine setting show perfectly the two faces of the Riding, the industrial and the pastoral, always closely linked.

The same thing is seen again in Saddleworth further south, where, despite the industry, it is evident that here was a part of the Riding which once perhaps could outdo even Bowland in natural beauty. The former urban district of Saddleworth was an area of 18,000 acres, half of them over 1,000 feet above sea level, an area of small hamlets scattered over valley bottom and hill top, among them the euphonic Diggle, Delph, Denshaw and Dobcross. Some hint of the area's former glory can be recognized by the traveller who journeys through it on the trans-Pennine railway which hugs the hillside high above the river Tame. From his carriage window he can look out on the 1,500-foot-high, rounded green hills which guard the mouth of the tributary Chew valley – Alphin Pike to the south and Pots and Pans, topped by the obelisk which is Saddleworth's war memorial, to the north. The best time to see Saddleworth is after heavy rain when the moorside cloughs are full of bright rushing water and the grass is at its greenest. One cannot overlook the area's industry of course, especially where comparatively thickly populated Greenfield and Uppermill, the district's former 'capital' run into one another, but in most parts of Saddleworth factories are small and built of the local stone, as are the majority of the houses, and there is enough building of good quality and rich in local character for some the villages to have been designated conservation areas. One feels it is a pity, though, that some of the restrictions on building which apply in a national park do not apply here, for the qualities the district has as a place to live in have been obvious to Manchester businessmen for some time, and new brick houses with wooden fascias, very much out of character with the locality, are strung out on the hillside on either side of Dobcross, an attractive village of stone-built weavers' cottages, while some very substantial modern houses obtrude outrageously on the moorland view from the high churchyard at Denshaw.

Some of the finest views in the district are from the Church Inn and the Cross Keys, two aptly named public houses – the keys are the symbol of St Peter – near to Saddleworth's parish church of St Chad in an isolated spot high up in a fold of hills away from the larger settlements and their industry. The Cross Keys is a splendid old place with the date 1745 over its door, a stone flagged kitchen to drink in, with a blazing fire in its Yorkshire range, and a 'two-holer' lavatory!

Saddleworth church has a mounting block and three-seater stocks dated 1698 by its gate. The present building dates from 1835, but there has been a church on the site since about 1200. Although isolated now, Saddleworth clough would have been the sensible place to build a church in the thirteenth century when the valley bottom was thickly wooded and most of the houses were among the hills. It was founded by the Stapletons, who held Saddleworth as tenants of the de Lacys, but was given by Roger de Lacy to Stanlaw Abbey in 1211. The monks of Stanlaw eventually moved to Whalley and for two and half centuries Saddleworth was one of 50 townships in the enormous Whalley parish. The monks took the local tithes and arranged for the church to be served by a priest from another of their churches, St Chad's, Rochdale. Of Saddleworth's own daughter churches, the oldest was St Thomas', which it was originally planned to build in the hamlet of Grange. Grange was the centre of Friarmere, one of four medieval administrative divisions of Saddleworth, or Quick as it was called in Domesday. The others were Quick Mere, Shaw Mere and Lord's Mere. By the 1760s, when St Thomas' was founded, Grange had declined in importance and the people of Denshaw, a growing hamlet of weavers, successfully petitioned for it to be built nearer to them at Heights. But in 1863 Denshaw got its own church and the chief settlement then served by Heights church was Delph, from whence access was not easy, particularly in bad weather. In 1884 St Hilda's mission church was founded at Delph, and now that church-going is not the popular activity it once was, the little bellcoted church 400 feet higher up in the hills has been closed and St Hilda's reconsecrated as the parish church of St Thomas, Friarmere.

There are two more eighteenth-century churches in Saddleworth. Holy Trinity at Dobcross, like a mill with two tiers of roundheaded windows, was consecrated in 1787, though its Italianate campanile was added in 1843. Although its clock has stopped, it is a prosperous looking place, for it draws a good congregation, particularly at Christmas when the Dobcross band accompanies the carol singing. The area under the gallery at the back has been screened off to form an attractive meeting room, and the font, a heavy Victorian affair, has been brought forward to stand just in front of the pulpit. It seems a pity that it is not a daintier piece of work which would fit better into this elegant Georgian interior with its beautiful ceilings tastefully decorated in yellow and white.

The third eighteenth-century church is St Anne's at Lydgate, a year younger than Holy Trinity. Here again are the two tiers of roundheaded windows in the local style of the period, and here too is a distinctive tower. This one, in a neo-Georgian style which seems to have been influenced by Art-Nouveau has a wavy top and dates from soon after the First World War. It is an attractive church in a lovely setting, a trim green garden, bright with yellow daffodils and pink rhododendrons in the springtime, with a long view of a winding lane which seems to beckon us over the moor.

The rest of Saddleworth's Anglican churches are Victorian, and some of them too have fine settings, especially tall-towered St Paul's, Scouthead, on a green bank high above the Oldham road, and nearly 1,000 feet above sea level. Christ Church, Friezeland is worth a visit, particularly by anyone who loves Victoriana, for were north aisle and transept not curtained and partly walled-off for vestries, it would be a perfect example of a High Victorian church interior. There are boards inscribed with the Ten Commandments on either side of an east window of garish 'back kitchen' glass with a great deal of gold about it, and chancel and sanctuary are paved with perfectly preserved patterned tiles. There are poppy-heads to the ends of the choir stalls, and an intricately carved and uncoloured royal coat-of-arms over the south door.

The churches of Saddleworth date from two periods when the local textile industry was prosperous, the late eighteenth century, the hey-day of the handloom weaver, and the second half of the nineteenth century, when the millowner was king. Cloth manufacture developed here, as elsewhere in the county, as a domestic industry because there was both rough pasture for sheep (and sheep farming was introduced into the area as long ago as the thirteenth century by the monks of Roche Abbey who had a grange at Grange) and soft water from the local gritstone for scouring the cloth. The making of woollens was combined with farming, the spinsters working at their wheels in the farmhouse producing yarn which their father and brothers would weave into cloth on their return from working in the fields. As the demand for cloth increased, work might be put out by the yeoman clothier at the farm to neighbouring cottagers. There are many fine examples of weavers' cottages in Saddleworth, a particularly good example being Streethouse near Tame Bridge. Such cottages usually have a long line of mullioned windows on the upper floor designed to give the weaver the maximum amount of light.

Sometimes the farm itself became the nucleus of a primitive factory, many of the textile processes being carried out on the same site. This is what happened at New Tame, between Denshaw and Delph, where a farmhouse known to have existed in 1642 has had other buildings built on at front and rear so that it itself is seen simply as two gable ends. The top storey of the farm building was rebuilt with a higher roof about 1780 to house handlooms, and a new set of mullioned windows was inserted. Adjoining buildings also have workrooms upstairs, extending their full width. The whole is a remarkable example of a cloth manufacturing community of just prior to the Industrial Revolution and the concentration of industry in the mills.

One process was difficult to carry out at home, and that was fulling – the pounding of cloth in soapy water with long wooden water-driven hammers until the fibres of wool hooked into one another and the cloth became thickened and felted. A fulling mill existed at Tame Bridge at least as early as 1728 and the building remains, part of premises now shared between a dye works and a sheet metal company. It was called the Walk Mill, for walker was another name for fuller and thus the trade was the origin of the common local surname Walker. By 1792 there were 72 waterwheels driving machinery along the banks of the Tame, but by this time two other processes had been factoryised: scribbling and carding. Scribbling involved breaking up the locks of wool to produce an even fleece and carding was the subsequent combing out of the wool into a long continuous sliver ready for spinning. Doing this type of work by hand was gradually superseded by the use of the carding engine, which consisted of a series of iron-toothed rollers. One of the earliest of Saddleworth's scribbling mills was Brownhill Bridge Mill, close to the Diggle Brook at the foot of Nicker Brow, Dobcross. With its small mullioned windows it is an excellent example of an early factory.

There is an example of a carding engine in Saddleworth's museum in the main street of Uppermill. It is only a small museum, run by members of the Saddleworth Historical Society, but it merits a visit, and the society deserve our support. Their pride in their lovely and interesting part of the county has led them to produce a number of valuable booklets, including some which are guides to what they call 'local interest trails', walks round what amounts to a large scale open-air museum of industrial archaeology, even though, unlike Coalbrookdale in Shropshire, it is not officially recognized as such.

The museum building was part of the Victoria Mill, a factory of the 1860s which for most of its life was used for cotton spinning. At the other end of the car park once stood High Street Mill which had one of the first steam engines in the area, while across the road is Alexandra Mill which also dates from the 1860s and manufactures flannel, something for which the area has long been famous. All these mills were close to the canal, now flanked by green lawns and made more attractive by the Muscovy ducks and mallard which glide across its waters, though once there was a busy wharf here on a waterway linking the Lancashire town of Ashton-under-Lyne with Huddersfield. The latter town was reached by way of the 3 mile, 135-yard-long Standedge tunnel, through which bargees propelled their boats by lying on their backs and pushing with their feet against the tunnel roof. One of the warehouses into which goods were unloaded from this important factor in Saddleworth's prosperity can be seen at Woolroad, close to the Navigation Inn. It served Stonebottom Mill, another factory which started life as a woollen scribbling mill in the late eighteenth century. From Woolroad in the 1830s two vessels sailed daily to London by way of the canal network. But roads were also important in maintaining Saddleworth's links with the outside world, and one of the original milestones of the Standedge–Oldham road constructed in 1792 stands close to the Navigation. It was the building of this road which made Uppermill the important centre which it is today. Later came the railway which, between Uppermill and Dobcross, spans the Tame Valley on a great viaduct.

Beneath the viaduct is the site of Mytholme Mill which existed in 1779 but closed in the 1880s. One can still see the mill race and the site of the waterwheel pit. The sites of these old mills are a source of great fascination to anyone interested in industrial archaeology. Close to Delph church is a children's playground, where the observant can trace the outline of a mill dam. It belonged to Woodhouse Mill, which specialized in fulling and dyeing from the mid-eighteenth century until it was burnt down in 1873. Just above the mill site is picturesque old Barley Bridge. It is a 'meal bridge', built by mill workers to earn money for their needs when there was a slump in the trade, and there were plenty of those, especially in the 1820s when a drought reduced the River Tame to a trickle and there was nothing to drive the mill machinery. This seems hard to believe today, especially when one sees the river after heavy rain; One of the most impressive sights in the district is the view from the bridge in Delph of the water pouring into its tributary Hull Brook from the tail race of Eagle Mill. (A tail race is the channel which returns water to the river after it has driven the mill wheel.)

Not all the mills which still remain intact are used for textile production today, particularly since the contraction of the cotton industry in the face of foreign competition. Slackcote Mills near New Tame, with a nice group of workers' cottages nearby, existed as fulling and carding mills in the 1780s but are now motor-car repair workshops. Wall Hill Mill, built in the 1790s, is now a metal works. In the 1840s its owners built the rows of tenter posts on the hillside above the A.62. Fulled cloth was attached to tenter hooks on such posts so that it would dry in the fresh air but not shrink. Another interesting survival is on a hillside near Delph church – a wool wall on which raw wool was laid out to dry after washing or dyeing.

Among the best-known manufacturers of textile machinery are Platt Brothers of Oldham. This firm was founded in the eighteenth century by the three sons of a blacksmith who lived at Bridge House, Dobcross. The house is still there, one of the most attractive buildings in a village of attractive buildings. It began life as a weaver's house; there is a through workshop on the upper floor and what were known as 'takin-in steps' leading up to it. It was the single-storey workshop next door which was the smithy and in it the brothers Platt manufactured carding engines for local mills. Later the Platts moved to Uppermill. Their workshop there, which they left on their move to Oldham in 1821, is now the Waggon Inn. Well known for its good food, it is, along with the museum, the Victoriana Café, the Saddleworth Pottery and the Saddleworth Sauna, one of those things which help to make industrial Uppermill almost a popular resort and the natural and historical attractions of the Saddleworth district deservedly better known.

16. & 17. *above* Temple Newsam, Leeds; *below* Bishopthorpe Palace, residence of the Archbishop of York.

CHAPTER FOUR

Kirklees

Until the construction of the M.62, the main road route from west of the Pennines to the heart of the West Riding was by the A.62 over Standedge Moor into the Colne Valley. And main line trains, having tunnelled through the hills, still pass along the valley on their way from Manchester to Leeds as they have done for 130 years. These West Riding valleys are not unlike those of South Wales. Smoke-blackened terraced houses line the main road, while the village centres lie away nearer the valley bottom; chapels are prominent in the landscape; and the people have a love of sport and music. (The Northern Union, which became the Rugby League, may be said to have originated in Huddersfield, and the Colne Valley Male Voice Choir has actually beaten the best Welsh choirs in the International Eisteddfod!) Here too green moorland provides a backdrop to the tall chimneys of industry. But while the Welsh chimneys are those of the pits, here of course they belong to the mills.

Probably the oldest mill in the whole of Kirklees – the metropolitan borough formed by the valleys of the Colne, the Holme, the Spen and their tributaries, by the valley of the Calder between Cooper Bridge and Horbury Bridge, by the moorlands of Emley and by Denby Dale – is the King's Mill on the banks of the Colne at Huddersfield. It has a history going back to the beginning of the twelfth century, when it belonged to the de Lacys, the then lords of the manor. From them it and the estate passed by marriage to the earls and dukes of Lancaster and then to the Crown – hence the name King's Mill. And although the oldest part was severely damaged by fire a few

18. & 19.   *above* Bramham Park from the south-west; *below* Harewood House, north front.

years ago, what was corn and fulling mill is still working as a producer of cloth for ladies' wear. The same is true of Colne Mills at Slaithwaite, the manorial mill of the Kayes of Woodsome Hall.

Although fulling had been done in the mills for hundreds of years there was much opposition among hand workers to the mechanization of other branches of the textile industry at the end of the eighteenth and beginning of the nineteenth century. This was particularly the case when cropping was mechanized. The hand croppers raised the nap of the cloth with teasels, a kind of thistle, and then removed the rough nap, which had the appearance of loose fur, with special shears to secure a smooth and even finish. But around 1790 a machine was invented which could be tended by one man and yet do the work of ten hand croppers. This was the shearing frame, which in the early years of the last century began to be installed in the mills of West Yorkshire. It was the time of the Napoleonic Wars, and there was already a good deal of unemployment owing to the loss of continental markets, while food prices were high due to bad harvests. The hand croppers, fearing for their own future, banded together and attacked places where the frames had been installed. Known as Luddites, a name whose origin is obscure but which had already been used by machinery breakers in the Nottingham area, they gathered on the night of 11 April 1812 at the Dumb Steeple, a column marking the boundary of the Kirklees Priory estate, which still stands at the junction of the A.62 and A.644, near where the Colne flows into the Calder. From there they marched on Rawfolds Mill at Liversedge. They failed to break into the mill, the owner, William Cartwright, having anticipated the attack since he had already lost valuable machinery in an ambush of the waggons bringing it to his factory over Hartshead Moor. He had slept above the mill with some of his employees, a number of soldiers and a guard dog, and they drove back the attackers who sufferred two fatalities. This event was the inspiration for Charlotte Brontë's novel *Shirley*.

Another book inspired by Luddite activities is Phyllis Bentley's *Inheritance*, which a few years ago was filmed in the Colne

Valley and became a popular television serial. It tells the story of a mill-owning family – the Oldroyds – which has been continued up to the present day in three other volumes. The central event of the early chapters is the murder by the Luddites of William Oldroyd, and it is based on fact. The original of William Oldroyd was William Horsfall, millowner of Marsden at the head of the Colne Valley, who had installed cropping frames at his mill and was shot on his way home from Huddersfield market along the old road which runs roughly parallel to A.62 over Crosland Moor. What was then open country is now a built-up area, and William Horsfall Street is near the site of the murder. Three of the four Luddites involved in the killing were employed in John Wood's cropping shop at Longroyd Bridge. It disappeared long ago and its site is now occupied by a bus garage. What does remain, however, is Milnsbridge House, the home of Joseph Radcliffe, the magistrate who made it his task to see that the murderers were caught and brought to trial. They were, and on the king's evidence of their fellow conspirator three of them were hanged at York. Radcliffe was rewarded with a baronetcy. His family left Milnsbridge soon after for Rudding Park near Harrogate. What was once their parkland is now covered by back-to-back houses and factories, and their fine classical mansion is used as a warehouse by a textile company and a firm of engineers. But there are other relics of Luddite days well cared for in Huddersfield's museum in Ravensknowle Park, including an example of the type of hammer used to smash machinery. It was known as Enoch, the name of the man who manufactured the shearing frames, and a Luddite slogan was 'Enoch makes them and Enoch breaks them'.

Also in the Huddersfield museum is a banner carried by the supporters of Richard Oastler, an early campaigner for the abolition of child labour in the mills. He was the land steward of the Thornhill family of Fixby Hall, now Huddersfield's golf club. He tried to get into Parliament but failed, so his good work was carried on there by his friend Michael Sadler, the M.P. for Aldborough, and by the famous Lord Shaftesbury. There is a reminder of the bad old days of factory slavery in

Kirkheaton churchyard, not far from Huddersfield. It is a column over the grave of 17 children, ten of them under 14 years old, who were accidentally burnt to death while engaged in night work at Atkinson's cotton mill, which still stands by the river at Colne Bridge.

In the Middle Ages Colne Valley cloth was taken to market at Almondbury, a hill-top village and suburb of Huddersfield which still has something of the air of a market town. Almondbury grew up under the protection of the de Lacy's castle on the reputed site of the ancient capital of the Brigantes. Castle Hill is a site which you would have to pay to see were it anywhere else but the 'mucky' West Riding. It is surrounded by a double bank of prehistoric earthworks and bisected by a ditch which the de Lacys constructed to protect their castle in the eleventh century. The well they used can still be seen, but the site of their keep is now occupied by a tower erected to commemorate Queen Victoria's Diamond Jubilee. The top of the tower is nearly 1,000 feet above sea level and the views from this the highest hill on a straight line west of the Urals are magnificent. On one side are the woodlands and pasture of the coal measures and on the other the bleak moorlands of the gritstone country, while far below, at the junction of the Colne and the Holme, is Huddersfield, not just a music hall joke, but the 'capital' of Kirklees and world famous centre of the worsted industry. The importance of the textile trade locally can be seen from the pages of advertisements in the *Huddersfield Examiner* for millworkers oddly described as teazers, doffers, greasy perchers, twister reelers, chain makers and cone winders.

When the days of feuding rival barons were long past, the local cloth market moved from Almondbury to Huddersfield, the natural route centre. In 1671, Sir John Ramsden, the lord of the manor, received a market charter from King Charles II. The original market cross still stands in the centre of town, with the arms of the Ramsdens and their marriage connections on its four sides. The founder of the family fortunes was William Ramsden of Greetland, a clothier and dealer in land who married the heiress of the Woods of Longley. His nephew, another William, bought Huddersfield from the Crown in 1599 and Almondbury a few years later. Old Longley Hall still stands in its rebuilt seventeenth-century form in Longley Road. The family's later house, New Longley, is now a special school and its park is a municipal golf course, soon to be turned into a residential estate for the students of the Huddersfield Polytechnic. The Ramsdens sold house and town to the corporation in 1920, but they are not likely to be forgotten. The town hall stands in Ramsden Street, and other street names like Fitzwilliam Street, Zetland Street, Dundas Street and Somerset Road commemorate their matrimonial links with noble families. The local technical college has been known both as the Ramsden and the Sir John Ramsden College and the arms of those Ramsdens who were lords of the manor are emblazoned in rich colour on the grand building in Railway Street where they collected their rents.

For a hundred years after the granting of Sir John's charter, cloth was displayed for sale on the tombstones and walls of the parish churchyard. The horses which brought it to town were stabled in inn yards like that of the aptly named Packhorse on the other side of Kirkgate. Unfortunately that handsome building was demolished a few years ago and replaced by part of a concrete shopping centre quite out of character with this basically eighteenth-century street. Other houses have had shop fronts put into them, but their character has not radically changed, although only Fleas, an inn of about 1750 at the bottom of the street, remains more or less intact.

In 1766 an undercover market was provided for the sale of cloth. The Cloth Hall did not last as long as the Packhorse, being demolished in 1929 to make way for the present A.B.C. cinema. Its clock tower was re-erected over a shelter in Ravensknowle Park.

The increase in population in the early nineteenth century and a boom in trade brought Huddersfield, served by canals and the turnpike roads which had replaced the packhorse tracks, prosperity and made it into what Friedrich Engels described as the most handsome manufacturing town in the North of England. Joseph Kaye, a talented local builder, put up fine new public buildings like the classical infirmary (now the main building of the Technical College) and the County Court in Queen Street, a handsome structure of 1825. His portrait, which shows him with a stove pipe hat on his head, a plan in his hand and a mill in the background, is in the art gallery on the top floor of Huddersfield's Public Library.

The streets laid out by Kaye for Huddersfield's bourgeoisie have fallen on hard times. Some have disappeared under a new ring road, while the most handsome of them, tree-lined Upper Spring Street, with its stone sets and its vista of the pedimented waterworks offices, now houses Commonwealth immigrants awaiting their turn to move to the suburban council estates. This has long been an immigrant area. The Poles were here before the West Indians and Pakistanis, and before them the Irish. The last were such good workers that the local manufacturers paid for nearby St Patrick's church, another of Kaye's buildings, to be erected for their use.

When the Irish moved in, the Huddersfield middle class moved out to the Halifax road. Here are terraces and semi-detached houses of the 1840s and 1850s, some Gothic in style and some classical. Here is the school they sent their sons to – Huddersfield College, built in 1838, complete with cloisters, and now an annex of the Tech.. Its most famous pupil was Herbert Henry Asquith, the son of a Morley manufacturer and a future prime minister. Another well-known old boy is Thomas Armstrong, who like Phyllis Bentley, wrote the saga of a millowning family, *The Crowthers of Bankdam*. Next-door to the school is the chapel the middle classes attended – the still fashionable Highfields, with Ionic pillars in front and the livery stables of the carriage folk behind.

In the 1860s and 1870s the millowners were building detached houses, some with Gothic towers, some with Italian campaniles, hidden behind laurels and rhododendrons on the Thornhill estate further up the road in leafy Edgerton. They had moved well away from their employees, whose fathers and their own had perhaps both started out in life as handloom weavers. Some of them, however, like the Brookes of Armitage Bridge, preferred to remain close to their mill and play the squire in the village they had created for their workers. The Brookes still own Armitage Bridge mill and, having been established in Honley as long ago as 1728, theirs is possibly the oldest family firm in England.

The house considered by most experts on architecture to be Edgerton's best is Banney Royd, designed by Lancashire architect Edgar Wood in a mock-Tudor Arts and Crafts style for a millionaire brewer around the turn of the century, and now a teachers' centre. There is other work by Wood, which is easily identified, in the neighbourhood of Banney Royd and especially in the village of Lindley, where among other things, he designed a row of artisans' cottages and an impressive public clocktower for the Sykes family of Acre Mills.

While Edgerton was being developed, important changes were taking place in Huddersfield's centre. A new shopping street, John William Street, named of course after a Ramsden, was constructed from the Market Place to St George's Square, which is now the subject of a preservation scheme and still one of the finest squares in the north of England. On one side is the railway station, designed by Pritchett of York and opened in 1847. Regarded as having the finest façade of any station building in England, its centre block has a portico on tall Corinthian columns and is linked by colonnades to small classical lodges on either side. These were the booking offices of the two companies which shared the station in its early days, the Lancashire and Yorkshire, and the Huddersfield and Manchester, and the companies' arms are picked out in colour on their pediments. Opposite the station is the Lion Arcade, a building of 1853 topped by a huge lion. (It is amazing how many lions there are on Huddersfield's late nineteenth-century buildings; the Estate Building, the old Library, the Conservative Club and the Town Hall all have them somewhere.) The other sides of the square are occupied by Huddersfield's premier hotel, the George, and Britannia Buildings, originally a warehouse but now the offices of the Huddersfield and Bradford Building Society, both of them splendid examples of Victorian secular architecture.

The Town Hall was one of the last important buildings to be

erected in Huddersfield in the last century. It is in two parts. The office block of 1876 is rather mean but the concert hall of 1881, which rises up behind it, is externally reminiscent of Second Empire Paris, and internally, for a public hall, sumptuously decorated. This is where the world famous Huddersfield Choral Society performs its annual *Messiah* and where culture-conscious Kirklees council puts on a whole season of concerts by internationally known orchestras. There is rarely a Saturday when there is not some sort of concert given either by organist, brass band, the Huddersfield Philharmonic Orchestra, or one of the several local choirs. There are lunchtime recitals on weekdays, and on two nights in the year hundreds of young instrumentalists from the orchestras of the local schools perform for their parents, ending with a sometimes discordant but always moving mass item.

The nineteenth century left Huddersfield still one of the most handsome towns in the north. Unfortunately the twentieth century has added little of architectural value and removed much. There are several undistinguished blocks of shops and offices, some hideous blocks of flats, a plain but functional civic centre, and the amazing public library and art gallery of about 1940 in a style which might best be described as civic Egyptian tempered by Third Reich. But the extension to the fine clock-towered Co-op of the 1890s made in 1936 and the Midland Bank, police station, court house and infirmary, all of the 1960s, are not without some merit, while the market hall is possibly the best of this century's additions to the town. Outside it, there is a terraced piazza where political speeches are made at election times and a large grassed area where the thousands of Saturday shoppers are entertained by one of the local brass bands or by Rag Day stuntmen from the Polytechnic. Around the corner is a pedestrian precinct used for other entertainments such as those provided by the White Rose Morrismen, and the loss of many early nineteenth-century town houses in this area has been at least partially compensated for by the cleaning of a lot of the buildings which remain to reveal the beauty of cream stone too long shrouded in industrial black. Moreover the natural beauty of the town's setting among the hills can now be appreciated better than ever from the splendid new ring road with its wide views and its verges ever bright with flowers.

Although Huddersfield is where the borough council meets, until adequate office space is provided in the town some departments will be accommodated in the handsome but strangely still unwashed Dewsbury town hall. Dewsbury lies about nine miles down stream from Huddersfield, beyond the junction of the Colne with the Calder. Between the two is Kirklees Park, the estate of the Armytage family, and the place which has given the new borough its name. Since it contains several towns of importance, notably Huddersfield, Dewsbury and Batley, as well as the lesser known but proud borough of Spenborough and urban districts of Heckmondwike, Holmfirth, Kirkburton, Mirfield, Colne Valley and Denby Dale, it is understandable that the new authority decided not to call itself by the name of any one of them. It seems odd, however, that it should have chosen that of a place which is actually just over the border in the neighbouring borough of Calderdale. Kirklees Park has, though, a significance in local legend. It is the site of Kirklees Priory, where, according to tradition, Robin Hood, having been bled by his wicked aunt, the prioress, shot his last arrow and was buried where it landed. Since local historians claim Robin of Sherwood as a native of the West Riding, it is perhaps not so surprising after all that the independently minded Yorkshire councillors should have chosen to call their borough after a place intimately associated with another independently minded 'tyke', just a little strange that the councillors of Calderdale did not think of it first.

Between Huddersfield and Dewsbury is the smaller township of Mirfield, a place of some importance to the ecclesiastical historian and the churchgoer. It has a rare medieval vicarage, the tower of a medieval church in the grounds of one by the famous Victorian firm of Gilbert Scott, the striking modern church of Christ the King replacing one recently destroyed by fire, a monastery of the Verona Fathers, and the mother house of the Anglican Community of the Resurrection. This order has had a number of famous members, notably in recent years Trevor Huddleston, the opponent of apartheid in South Africa, and Geoffrey Beaumont, the composer of twentieth-century hymn tunes. The twin green roofed towers of the community church up on its cliff top dominate this part of the Calder valley. In its Romanesque chancel are buried the ashes of the order's founders, Bishop Gore of Oxford and Bishop Frere of Truro. Its grounds contain a theological college, and on one day in July, Commemoration Day, when Gore and Frere and the founders of other monastic communities are remembered and addresses are given by famous preachers, the lanes round about are packed with the coaches in which vicars and rectors have brought their parishioners to share in the services and bunfights at their old college.

Dewsbury, famous for its blankets, has also played an important rôle in church history. Indeed its bulky, largely eighteenth- and nineteenth-century parish church stands on what is probably the most sacred spot in the West Riding. By tradition St Paulinus preached here in 627, having come north with Princess Ethelburga of Kent on her marriage to King Edwin of Northumbria, and baptized thousands in the Calder. Dewsbury church was mentioned in Domesday Book as the church of a parish of 400 square miles, and medieval parishes like those of Huddersfield, Almondbury, Kirkheaton and Kirkburton were carved out of it. However, as in most industrial regions, the majority of the churches of the textile belt are nineteenth-century, put up – some with the aid of part of a government grant of one million pounds given to commemorate the victory of Waterloo – in order to serve a growing population which could not be accommodated in the ancient parish churches.

Notable among the 'Waterloo' churches is Emmanuel, Lockwood. For one thing it was built in the wrong place; its plans were somehow accidentally swapped for those of All Saints', Netherthong, designed by the same architect, Dennis Chantrell. Chantrell, although working in the 1820s and '30s at a time when English church architecture is generally considered to have been undistinguished, made a very important

100

contribution to the West Riding scene, and his buildings are full of interesting detail. One of his favourite building materials was a relatively new and relatively cheap one, iron. At Lockwood, where the church is nearer his original design that at Netherthong, which was remodelled in 1877, he used iron girders for the nave pillars which he then had cased in wood and painted so that they looked like plastered stone. Lockwood church, incidentally, is one of the few where the tradition is continued of breaking the Lenten fast by giving the congregation simnel-cake on Refreshment (or Mothering) Sunday in the middle of the penitential season.

The shops in the main street of Lockwood, Bridge Street, were built around the same time as the church and although some are empty now they still have an aura of former opulence about them, for they date from the time when Lockwood, now a suburb of Huddersfield, was a spa. But the little classical bath house is now part of an engineering works, and the hotel where people stayed when they came to take the waters was till recently the home of *Speedyfro* frozen foods.

Many of the nineteenth-century churches were built by manufacturers for their workpeople or in memory of members of their families. The Brookes, for example, employed Chantrell to build St Paul's, Armitage Bridge, and the church of St Thomas the Apostle was erected by the Starkeys to designs by Sir Gilbert Scott across the road from their mill at Longroyd Bridge in 1859. But perhaps the most interesting of such churches are those belonging to the group founded by the Brook family of Meltham Mills. James Brook, a member of the firm of cotton thread manufacturers Jonas Brook and Brothers, built the first, St James at Meltham Mills itself. In 1857, on the day of the funeral there of another member of the family, Charles John Brook, there was a terrific storm, but it is said that as the coffin was being lowered a lull was heralded by the appearance of a rainbow and it was decided to build another church to his memory at the rainbow's end. This was Christ Church, Helme in a beautiful wooded hillside setting, half-a-mile from St James'. Helme church is unusual in these parts in having a shingled spire, and each shingle is inscribed with the name of someone who answered an appeal to people called Helme for money for its resoration. There is writing on the inside walls too, almost every available space being painted with a scriptural text.

Until the 1930s the same was true of St Mary's, Wilshaw, the most amazing of the three churches. From the outside it looks to be a church of reasonable size, if of a peculiar architectural style with its capped 'French Canadian' type central tower. But open the main door under the tower and you will find yourself in a vestibule containing two marble busts, one of a bald bewhiskered Victorian gentleman, the other of a lady of the same period. A door on the left leads into what is in fact quite a small church, one on the right into a school room containing no less than five oil paintings of members of a Victorian family, a room which, with what was once a vicarage, makes up the rest of this remarkable piece of architecture – not just a dual purpose, but a triple purpose building of 1863. The bewhiskered gentleman is the builder of the church, the Brook brothers' nephew, Joseph Hirst; the woman is his wife, Eleanor Ramsey and the pictures are of them and their family. Himself a millowner, the present vicarage was Hirst's house, and the village largely his creation.

From Wilshaw a lane which passes a row of houses with what is surely one of the loveliest of street names, Calmlands, leads to the small Pennine town of Meltham. Meltham church has an interesting history. Although the present building is substantially of the eighteenth century, the first church on the site was consecrated in 1651 by the Bishop of Elphin, an Irish diocese, and was one of very few Anglican churches founded during the time of the Commonwealth. Its date-stone is in the porch of the present building, and some of its windows are now in a cottage across the road.

Not much remains of eighteenth-century parish church architecture in the district, but there are one or two imposing chapels, notably the Baptist Chapel at Lockwood of 1792 with its Venetian window and Tuscan porch, although it was partially reconstructed about 1850. Only one classical pillar is left of the old church at Longwood in the churchyard of its successor. Slaithwaite church was built in 1788, almost in the style of a mill like its contemporaries in Saddleworth. Holmfirth church is of a similar date and not of great interest though it stands in a very interesting little town. Although many miles from the Dales, it was described in the *Radio Times* as a typical Dales town when it was picked as the setting for the popular comedy series, *The Last of the Summer Wine*. And indeed it looks the part. Halfway up the Holme valley, beneath the wild moorland of Holme Moss, it is, despite being only six miles from Huddersfield, so much out on a limb and the centre of its own little world as to exhibit a sturdy independence. It has its own street illuminations at Christmas time, and very impressive they are too. And it has its own anthem, *Pratty Flowers,* which has been recorded on a disc by Holmfirth Rotary Club. Its chorus is all about fighting 'yon French and Spaniards'. The Napoleonic wars must have had a profound effect on Holmfirth; it must be one of very few places to have a memorial column to the conclusion of the temporary Peace of Amiens in 1802.

Holmfirth used to be in the parish of Kirkburton. Kirkburton has possibly the most perfectly medieval church in the district. Although the east end is nineteenth-century, most of the building is over 700 years old and looks it; the nave has six Early English arches on octagonal pillars and is crammed with Elizabethan, Jacobean and Georgian pews. Almondbury church, rebuilt between 1470 and 1522 and restored in the 1870s, also contains some splendid old woodwork, notably a towering Tudor font cover and a splendid oak ceiling carved with a poem about the Passion and dated 1522. Huddersfield's parish church of 1836 is the third to occupy the present site, and most of Kirkheaton's was rebuilt last century, but the fifteenth-century tower and the Beaumont chapel survive from an earlier building. The Beaumonts of Whitley, ancestors of the former president of the Liberal Party, are one of the few families who actually did come over with the Conqueror, but not all the numerous Kirklees people who bear that name have Norman blood (at least, not in the direct male line). In the style of the Scottish clans the name was adopted by the family's tenants and retainers. Nothing remains of the old hall at Whitley Beaumont and the estate has been ravaged by open-cast coal mining, for this is the area where the coal and woollen districts meet.

The mining village of Emley is overshadowed by Europe's tallest concrete structure, a 900-foot tower topped by a 180-foot television mast, its top 185 feet lower than that of its steel predecessor which blew down in a gale and partially demolished a chapel. Close by is Denby Dale, the home of another monster that went wrong – a huge pie baked to commemorate Queen Victoria's Golden Jubilee which was found to be bad when opened. The first Denby Dale Pie was baked in 1788 to celebrate George III's recovery from his mental affliction; the most recent, which weighed over six tons, in 1964 to celebrate six royal births.

There is another impressive landmark at Emley besides the television mast – the tall tower of its church, over 400 years old. The living is in the gift of Lord Savile, who regularly reads one of the lessons at the Sunday service. The tombs of the Saviles and their ancestors the Thornhills are in their fifteenth-century chantry chapel in Thornhill church. They were loyal to King Charles in the Civil War and their house at Thornhill was destroyed by Parliament, but the moat is still there. The same fate befell another Savile seat, Howley Hall near Batley. The Saviles' predecessors at Howley, the Mirfields, founded a chantry in Batley parish church in 1482. The church is still largely a fifteenth-century building and has some medieval stained glass.

But Batley, the centre of the shoddy trade – the manufacture of cloth from recovered fibres from the rags collected by the rag and bone men – has little else to recommend it to the visitor. It is one of the most run-down of the Yorkshire manufacturing towns, and is probably best known for its Variety Club, often the resort of cinema, radio and television stars whose fame has begun to fade. Other exotic features of Batley are the palm trees which grow alongside the Heckmondwike road and a remarkable collection of *Chinoiserie* in the town's museum.

Batley was one of two municipal boroughs to be incorporated in Kirklees. The other was Spenborough, itself made up of the Spen valley townships of Cleckheaton and Liversedge. It is an area well known in the industrial world for its textile machinery and for its blankets, and, like other parts of Kirklees, in the world of literature for its connections with the Brontë family. Liversedge church was founded by Hammond Roberson, the original of the Rev. Matthewman Helstone in *Shirley*. The Elizabethan Oakwell Hall at Birstall, a little to the north of Liversedge, also features in the book as Fieldhead, and is open to the public. Another old house in the area which is now a museum is Red House at Gomersal which was featured in *Jane Eyre* as Briarmains, the home of Hiram Yorke, while The Rydings at Birstall is said to be the Thornfield Hall of the same book. Charlotte Brontë knew Birstall well because it was the home of her school friend Ellen Nussey and of their teacher Margaret Wooler, both of whom are buried in the churchyard. All three Brontë sisters attended Roe Head School at Mirfield, and Anne returned to the village to be a governess at Blake Hall, where she worked out the plot of *Agnes Grey*. There are strong Brontë associations too in the neighbouring metropolitan boroughs of Bradford and Calderdale.

CHAPTER FIVE

Calderdale

The boundary between Kirklees and Calderdale lies along a Pennine ridge, which is crossed by the A.629, the road linking the capitals of the two districts, Huddersfield and Halifax, at a point called Ainley Top. On one side of the Ainleys, where the road has sometimes been blocked by the winter snows, they read the *Examiner* and follow the fortunes of Huddersfield Town; on the other they support Halifax Town and take the *Courier*. The road was built about 1820. A few hundred yards to the east is the Halifax Old Road, constructed by Blind Jack of Knaresborough in 1777. His road was meant to cope with industrial traffic carrying increasingly heavy loads and he provided a much better and firmer surface than was previously the case. If you want to see what a road was like before the turnpike companies employed men like Blind Jack to build their toll roads you have only to travel a couple of miles east to just beyond where the present Huddersfield–Bradford road (A.641) runs over the boundary ridge and down into Brighouse. Parallel to it is Shepherds Thorn Lane. It looks like a farm track, but before the present road was constructed this was a major route, a fact betrayed by a raised pavement at the side of the lane near where it passes the entrance to Bradley Wood, the site of an ironworks managed by the monks of Fountains. The pavement is what is known locally as a *causey* or causeway, and gave a sure footing to packhorses carrying wool to the manufacturer or finished cloth to market. Their normal load was carried in two panniers, each holding 120lb of goods. In early household and trading accounts *load*, meaning 240lb is

20. Leeds Town Hall.

frequently used as a measure instead of our hundredweight or stone, for, in addition to carrying wool and cloth, the pack animals brought the householders coal and salt. Salt was of vital importance as a means of keeping meat fresh, and the Calderdale place name of Salterhebble is said to indicate that the village lay along a salt road from the mines of Cheshire. The men who drove the packhorses were known as 'jaggers', hence the frequency with which the street name Jagger Lane occurs in West Yorkshire.

Some of the inns which provided the jaggers with refreshment still stand; a few of them also served as coaching inns when road improvements had taken place. One of them is the Mount Skip at Wadsworth, built in 1718 alongside a remote lane which was then a main route from Halifax into Lancashire. Another is the Nag's Head at Ainley Top, one of the few places where they continue the old Yorkshire custom of providing lunch-time visitors with free bread and dripping. At one time diners at the inn would have had a panoramic view of the Calder valley; today they can see little more than a long succession of vehicles careering up and down the M.62 motorway, which has recently been built along the ridge and which follows in places a very ancient route, that taken by a Roman road between forts at Ilkley and Manchester. It actually crosses the site of a fort locally at Slack, near the village of Outlane. Other major roads carrying east-west traffic, and now partly superseded by the motorway, run alongside the River Calder far below in the valley bottom. These originated, if not in packhorse tracks, in eighteenth- and nineteenth-century turnpike roads, like the ones Blind Jack built. Here and there one can still see the original milestones and spot the toll houses built by the turnpike companies. There is one at Steanor Bottom near Todmorden which still has the different tolls inscribed on it, and is being restored.

The increasing need for a reliable way of carrying bulky goods led to turnpike companies finding themselves with rivals in the form of canal companies. As early as 1698, the Calder had been made navigable as far as Wakefield; in 1740 a group of Halifax businessmen employed a surveyor to prepare a

21.   F. L. Pearson's retro-choir, Wakefield Cathedral.

scheme to extend navigation further upstream. The scheme came to nothing, but in 1757 a further survey was made by the Yorkshire engineer Smeaton, of Eddystone lighthouse fame, and by 1765 the Calder and Hebble Navigation had been completed as far as Salterhebble, using the path of the rivers where practicable and artificial cuts elsewhere. It was not until 1828, however, that the canal was extended a further two miles up the Hebble valley towards the centre of Halifax, with a new terminus at Bailey Hall. Meanwhile branch canals had been constructed from Cooper Bridge to Huddersfield (the Sir John Ramsden Canal), and from Salterhebble along the Calder valley to Sowerby Bridge, where the wharves became the centre of a new town with Wharf Street as its principal thoroughfare. Till recently the canal basin here was virtually derelict, but now it is the starting point of narrow boat holiday cruises which are booked up long before the season begins.

The Sowerby Bridge branch was completed in 1767; by 1802 the canal system had been extended even further up the valley, through Hebden Bridge and across the Pennines to Rochdale. There would not have been much besides inns at Hebden Bridge, an important route centre, before the canal came and industry was attracted to its banks. By 1820 steam power had come to the district and a new mill village had begun to replace the older settlement of handloom weavers on the hill to the north as the commercial centre of the township of Heptonstall.

Heptonstall is now a museum piece, a splendid example of a Pennine textile village of the days before the factory system took root. On sunny weekends, visitors wander about with the Calder Civic Trust guidebook in their hands, inspecting the village pump and pinfold, the remains of the stocks and the lock-up, the oldest cloth hall in Yorkshire and the oldest Methodist chapel in the world, its foundation stone laid by John Wesley himself in 1764. And of course there are lots of weavers' cottages.

The old houses of Calderdale are full of interest. Many of them were built by yeoman clothiers and reflect the prosperity the wool trade brought them in the sixteenth and seventeenth centuries. Not all are still private dwellings; several have been converted into inns. One of these is the Fleece at Elland, built in 1610 and said to contain a bloodstain which cannot be erased. Kershaw House at Luddenden Foot is now used for so-called 'Tudor' banquets, where mead is drunk, and there is entertainment by jovial jesters, music from merry minstrels, service from buxom wenches, and even a dancing bear. Dated 1650, it exhibits something which is a distinctive feature of the large houses of its period in the area – a rose window above the doorway to its porch. The oldest of these windows was in the original Heath Grammar School at Halifax, built between 1597 and 1601. Fortunately, when a new school was built in 1878, the window was retained. There is another rose window at Barkisland Hall. Built in 1638, the Hall is used by Lord Kagan, manufacturer of Harold Wilson's Gannex mackintoshes, to entertain visiting businessmen. Its furnishings include a splendid collection of chess sets, one in the likeness of the Tory and Labour front benches of the 1960s, and the cushions on some of its chairs are covered with tartan raincoat lining. The Hall is just one of a number of sixteenth- and seventeenth-century houses in the village. Another is the Griffin Inn of 1642. A mile or so along the road is Ripponden in the valley of the Ryburn, a tributary of the Calder. Here is what is claimed to be one of the oldest inns in Yorkshire, the Old Bridge, which actually stands by a packhorse bridge. Known to have existed in 1313, its shape, the slope of the floor, and the different levels on which it is built make it seem almost like a fun fair crazy house. In the lower bar a splendid example of a cruck beam has been exposed.

Another of Calderdale's many interesting inns, the Spring Rock at Greetland, is a centre for one of Yorkshire's most unusual pastimes – knur and spell. Sometimes called 'poor man's golf', it involves hitting the knur, a marble-sized ball made of clay, as far as possible, using a stick with a head measuring two inches by three. The spell is not the stick but the equipment which holds the ball before it is hit. It is either a cup on a spring which shoots the knur into the air when it is released, or it is a kind of gallows with the knur in a noose on the end of a lace. In South Yorkshire the game is known as nipsy.

At one time public houses occasionally included libraries among their amenities. The seventeenth-century Lord Nelson at Luddenden, which, re-named after Trafalgar, was originally the White Swan, had a library of 1,000 volumes, some of which are now in Sowerby Bridge public library. Sobriety and decorous conduct were required of members, and drunkenness and swearing cost the culprit 2d for each offence. One wonders how much was paid by the Brontës' brother Branwell when he was a member, for, although he was a witness to other people signing the pledge of the temperance society of which his father was president, he was a notorious drunkard. He was a booking clerk at Luddenden Foot station, the railway joining the turnpike and canal along the Calder valley, and depriving them of much of their business, in 1840. Branwell Brontë was dismissed by the railway company in March 1842, after less than two years service, for being careless in keeping his accounts. He had earlier been moved from Luddenden Foot to Sowerby Bridge station, though the reason is not clear.

Several places in the area have Brontë connections. Partly fifteenth-century, timber built Shibden Hall is said to have been the Thrushcross Grange of *Wuthering Heights,* and features of a neighbouring house, High Sunderland, were incorporated in Emily's description of Wuthering Heights itself. High Sunderland has gone, but some of its painted timbers are in Halifax's museum at Bankfield, along with a reproduction of one of its wall paintings. Also in the museum are parts of other old houses, but there is nothing from Shibden Hall because it is itself now a museum, splendidly furnished with antiques.

Shibden Dale is delightful, although it is not far from the factories of Halifax and Bradford, and in one of its most pleasant spots is the Shibden Mill Inn. Over 400 years old, it is close to the bubbling stream that once drove the wheel of a corn-mill which stood on the site of the present car park. It is a lovely, well-run old house, one of the best places to enjoy a good meal or relax over a drink in the whole of the Riding.

Another lovely valley is Cragg Vale, once the 'kingdom' of 'King David' – David Hartley, leader of the infamous Cragg Vale coiners. At a time when English gold was in short supply, the Government legalized certain foreign coins for circulation. It was one of these, the Portuguese 4,000 reis piece of 1722, which was couterfeited in Cragg Vale. It was made from clippings from guineas lent to the coiners by dishonest aquaintances at two shillings a time. The counterfeit coins were given only 22 shillings' worth of gold but passed for 27. Eventually the local supervisor of Customs and Excise, William Dighton, got enough evidence about the coiners through a paid informer to have Hartley arrested on 14 October 1769, while he was drinking in the Old Cock in Halifax. This sixteenth-century former town house of the Saviles still stands in Southgate, the town's pleasant pedestrian precinct. Hartley's arrest was followed by Dighton's murder, possibly because some influential people feared that they might be discovered to be accessories and ruined. Joseph Hanson, the deputy constable of Halifax, was actually arrested but managed to escape from custody. Robert Thomas and Matthew Normanton were charged with Dighton's murder, but were set free because of insufficient evidence. However, when fresh evidence came to light they were re-arrested and this time charged with highway robbery, for Dighton's pockets had been rifled. They were found guilty and hanged at York. Afterwards their bodies were suspended in chains from a specially constructed gallows on 864-foot-high Beacon Hill, which dominates Halifax on its eastern side, their arms outstretched and fingers pointing towards Bull Close Lane, where the murder had been committed. By this time, Hartley had already been executed and buried in Heptonstall churchyard, where his grave can still be seen.

A little over a hundred years earlier, the authorities in Halifax were chopping off criminals' heads. Yorkshire thieves had their own litany, 'From Hell, Hull and Halifax, good Lord deliver us', and it is said that the thing they feared most in Halifax was the gibbet – a 'guillotine' used in the West Riding long before the French Revolution. 52 people are known to have been executed by it between 1541 and 1650. The blade which beheaded them is in Bankfield museum; the stone platform on which the gibbet stood is in a square of newly seeded lawn at the junction of Gibbet Street and Bedford Street North, and a reconstruction of the machine, with blade permanently fixed, has been erected over it. Only one man, John Lacy, is known to have escaped the gibbet. He did so by crossing over the Hebble, the town boundary, but after living in safety for seven years he foolishly returned to Halifax and was caught and executed on 29 January 1623. In 1971, Tetley's brewery commemorated him in the name of a new public house, The Running Man.

Another curiously named new inn is the Pot o' Four. Its name is derived from the pot in which metal hand combs were heated before being used to comb out the long-stapled wool from which worsted cloth is made. Some pots held three combs, others were pots of four. A large number of public house names in the area reflect the local importance of the wool trade. The Fleece, the Woolpack, the Slubbers' Arms (slubbing is the process of joining together the slivers of carded wool before twisting them to make a soft thread for spinning), the Yarn Spinner and the Shears all occur within a few miles of Halifax.

Among the oldest of Halifax's hostelries is the Ring o' Bells, next door to the parish church, one of the few remaining relics of medieval Halifax, standing very forlornly in what was at one time the centre of the town, surrounded by decaying warehouses and demolition sites. One of them has enough tufts of grass for a flock of sheep to be put out to graze on it. Nearby, dead rats lie on the pavement beneath a wall inscribed DON'T VOTE in foot-high whitewashed letters. But the inside of the Ring o' Bells, which has views of what has gone on its walls, is cosy, and the interior of the parish church is magnificent. Both were built in the fifteenth century. (Elland church, about two miles away, is fifteenth-century too, with glass of the same period in its east window.) There is much impressive woodwork in Halifax church, including a magnificent spire-shaped font cover as old as the church itself, the fine communion rail of 1698, and choir stalls with grotesque heads on their bench-ends and carvings, including one of a pelican feeding her young with her own blood, under their seats. The nave and chapels are full of box pews (many of them genuine seventeenth-century work, but some of them copies) with little knobs on their ends and flowers carved on their doors. The windows too are full of interest. In the north and south choir aisles the lozenged and star-patterned leading around the clear glass dates from Cromwell's time.

The south choir aisle is the chapel of the Duke of Wellington's regiment. Their regimental museum is at Bankfield, where one can see the battle of Waterloo being fought out in lights on a screen above a case containing Wellington's telescope and one each of his and Napoleon's shirts. Nearby are lamps taken from Napoleon's carriage and hair from the tail of the Iron Duke's horse, Copenhagen.

Close to the regiment's chapel in Halifax church, under a rose window, is a tablet with a carving of the Good Samaritan by the famous sculptor Westmacott and an inscription to the memory of John Rawson, whose life was spent 'earnestly endeavouring to follow the example of his blessed saviour, who went about doing good'. The Rawsons were a banking family. In the street named after them is a house built in 1766 for another banker, John Royds. A low line of mean shops obscures its ground floor from the street, but above them can be seen some of the magnificent work of the well-known Yorkshire architect, John Carr – a central pedimented block of three bays, with projecting wings. This was once the garden front of the house. The other side, in spacious George Street, which might more appropriately be called a square, has been altered and the colonnade in the part occupied by the Huddersfield and Bradford Building Society is only neo-Georgian. But there are other impressive Georgian houses in the town, most of them unfortunately in a sad state of disrepair. Some may indeed have been demolished by the time you read this book. No. 23 Savile Road is one of the best preserved. A large, almost mansion-like building, completed in 1791, one of its wings was a warehouse for the wool merchants who lived there. Just below it, nearer to the town centre, is Kirby Leas, a fine early nineteenth-century house, but unfortunately it has been deserted. Its upstairs windows and fanlight have been smashed, the downstairs windows have been boarded up, and dandelions flourish in its flower beds. A handsome Georgian terrace in Clare Road also appears to have been abandoned, yet in some towns the houses in it would be very desirable residences indeed. However, Hopwood Hall in Hopwood Lane, just above Lewin's public house, whose sign tells us it was established in 1769, has a new lease of life as a branch of the Abbey National Building Society. These once fine town houses were built in a period of considerable prosperity for Halifax, a prosperity which was reflected in the building of a number of handsome classical churches in the neighbourhood, including Holy Trinity in Harrison Road, erected between 1795 and 1798. It has a domed tower and is unusual in having its main entrance at the side of the altar and in being square in shape. Of the other churches of the same period in Calderdale, perhaps the most notable is St Matthew's at Rastrick, now run jointly by the Anglicans and the Methodists.

The finest of the eighteenth-century buildings in Halifax is undoubtedly the Piece Hall, the cloth hall of 1778, a building constructed round a vast courtyard of 10,000 square yards, with pillared galleries all the way round opening into 315 rooms meant for cloth manufacturers to display their wares in. Over its main gateway at the foot of Westgate is a classical cupola supported by a wooden colonnade. It contains a bell used to signify the beginning and end of business, and is topped with a golden fleece and weathervane. As the number of factories grew and the domestic industry began to decline, and it was possible for a buyer to travel round two or three mills, see all the cloth he needed, and have the pieces directly transported home, there was no longer any need for the double journey of cloth down to the Piece Hall and out again. In 1871, therefore, the hall became a wholesale fruit and vegetable market, and such it remained for a hundred years. Now the building has been restored, and various parts of it contain local government offices, a café, antique shops, an art gallery and an industrial museum. The east end of the courtyard has been grassed over and is used as a pedestrian precinct and exhibition centre, whilst the paved west end accommodates a twice weekly open market.

116

The nearby Borough Market is a magnificent building of the 1890s in French Renaissance style. Inside, it is like a cathedral of glass and iron, with walls and columns tastefully painted in primrose, lichen, orange and white. In the middle, an iron clock stands beneath a great glass dome.

Halifax is full of splendid nineteenth-century buildings, so many of them that individual buildings do not fix themselves in the memory in the way they do at Huddersfield, where the Victorian town centre is smaller. One building is, however, unforgettable – the marvellous Town Hall designed by Sir Charles Barry, architect of the Houses of Parliament, its fine tower completing an impressive vista along Corn Market and Princess Street from Southgate's pedestrian precinct. It is neighboured by the handsome White Swan Hotel, in the style of a High Victorian London club, and a street away is the towered post office of 1887. This stands in the commercial heart of the town, along with a number of dignified banks, and close by are the enormous new headquarters of the world's biggest building society.

Big though the central business district of the town undoubtedly is, Halifax does not seem at first sight to have anywhere near as many shops as its neighbour and rival, Huddersfield, but this is because a large number of them are contained in arcades like the Arcade Royale, the Albany Arcade and Princes Arcade. These arcades are one of the most attractive features of a very handsome town; another is the way several of the street are paved with sets laid down in patterns, continental fashion.

Halifax has some fine Victorian churches, the best of the lot being All Souls', Haley Hill, designed by Sir Gilbert Scott for a worsted manufacturer, Colonel Edward Akroyd. Its spire dominates Dean Clough on the north side of town, standing as it does high above the complicated network of bridges and fly-overs that would otherwise be the most prominent feature in the scene. Its limestone facing has not stood up well to the smoky atmosphere and it is crumbling away, but the church is still very impressive, its walls a paler shade of grey than anything near it. Scott said it was his best church. On its south side

is a statue of Akroyd, looking over the road to his mills. Round
about are the terraces of houses put up for his workpeople, not
to be rented but to be bought through a special scheme
arranged with the then new Halifax Building Society. They
were much better built and had far better amenities than most
working class dwellings of the time. Akroyd had already built a
model factory village, with a school and a library, at Copley on
the south bank of the Calder, where he had a canteen shed in
which 600 workmen were served dinners of meat and potatoes
at 2d a time. It is the Colonel's house on Haley Hill, Bankfield,
which is now the town's museum, and few museums have such
an impressive entrance as this one – a staircase between walls
painted with pictures of Roman gods, lit by crystal chandeliers.
It looks as if it ought to be lined with bewigged flunkeys. On the
other side of the road is a Gothic stable block, still with its
cobbled yard, but its buildings accommodating firms of paper
merchants and undertakers, not horses.

Filling the valley bottom below this remarkable village of
Akroydon are the mills of one of Halifax's most famous
firms – Crossley's, the carpet manufacturers – their Italianate
towers proclaiming the fact that they were built in 1857. Both
Halifax and Brighouse are world famous for their carpets. As
long ago as 1770, blue carpets were being made especially for
sale in Guinea; they were wrapped in oil-cloth painted with
negroes and elephants 'in order to captivate the natives.' Like
Colonel Akroyd, the Crossleys built a magnificent church,
Square Congregational, with a 235-foot-high spire. In 1971 it
was damaged by fire, and now the enormous building is in
ruins, looking as if the demolition men had found its destruction too formidable a task and had abandoned it. Next-door, in
that miserable area close to parish church and railway station,
is its dilapidated predecessor, a brick chapel of 1772. The
Crossley family also built an estate for their workers (again
with the aid of the building society) on the opposite side of the
valley from Akroydon, their Liberal sympathies betrayed by
the names of streets commemorating heroes of the Parliamentary side in the Civil War – Hampden Place, Milton Street and
Cromwell Street. Others are named after members of the

family, Francis Street and Florence Street. Here and there are the more exotic names introduced into the Crossleys' kingdom in the second half of the twentieth century – the Kashmir Food Store, the Sijad Trading Company, the Shahid Food Store, and Chani's Place. And yet, despite the names and the dark faces, one somehow expects to see clogs and shawls among the smoke-blackened stonework of working class Halifax, and it is not the surprise it might be elsewhere to find clogs amongst the 'Quality Footware' sold in B, Aaron and Son (estd. 1810)'s shop close to castellated North Bridge.

Among the blackest buildings in Halifax, where the town centre is nearly all newly cleaned light brown stone, are Sir Francis (Frank) Crossley's almshouses, built in 1855 with Gothic towers at either end. They are overlooked at the back by Sir Frank's own house, Belle Vue, which now houses the public library. Across the road from it, beyond the Halifax cenotaph, is the People's Park he gave to the town, laid out by Sir Joseph Paxton, who designed the Crystal Palace. Among its statues of classical gods is one of Sir Frank himself, put up by his grateful fellow citizens. It is sheltered by an Italianate pavilion inscribed 'The rich and poor meet together – the Lord is maker of them all.' Another of the Crossleys, Joseph, gave Halifax a further set of almshouses, built in the Tudor style round a very large open quadrangle off Arden Road between 1863 and 1870. The family also founded the orphanage which is now Crossley and Porter School. It stands at the edge of Savile Park, a vast open common of trim lawns, Halifax's answer to Harrogate's Stray, ending in a cliff-top promenade with fine views over the Calder valley, close to the area of big middle class houses which is the town's equivalent of Huddersfield's Edgerton. Here too is the curious Wainhouse Tower. All sorts of legends have grown up as to why the 253-foot-high, eight-sided, minaret-like tower was put up between 1871 and 1875. One is that John Edward Wainhouse, who built it, wanted to see over the wall of a neighbour he disliked, Sir Henry Edwards. In fact it shrouds the chimney built for Wainhouse's dye-works down in the valley below. If you inspect the base of the tower you can see where the flue was meant to enter. Before the chimney was completed, Wainhouse had sold the dye-works but its new owner did not want the chimney so it was converted into an ornamental tower, with 403 steps leading up between the chimney and the stone casing to the top, and two balconies for veiwing the surrounding scene en route. (It belongs to Calderdale council now, and is open to the public two days in May and two in September.) It is an incredible structure, said to have been put together on the 'mortice and tenon' principle without mortar. Near the tower is the site of the quarry from which the stone for it came. The Halifax–Huddersfield area is rich in quarries, and local millstone grit, being resistant to sea-water erosion, was exported for harbour works at such places as Bombay, Calcutta, Hong Kong, Sydney and Copenhagen. Halifax stone was used too for the War Office and extensions to the British Museum, while Elland flags have paved streets throughout the land.

Wainhouse Tower is one of the surprises of Calderdale. Perhaps the biggest surprise of all in what is generally thought of as an industrial area is the green valley of the Hebden Water, a pleasant, wooded and sheltered spot, contrasting considerably with the bleak and windy moors above, where an obelisk commemorating the defeat of Napolean stands 1,400 feet up on Stoodley Pike. The valley is National Trust property, and a two-mile nature trail through the woods will lead you to Hardcastle Crags, a huge mass of rocks with one of the district's most splendid views. This valley has been adopted by exiled Swiss as an area which reminds them of home, and once a year the Swiss flags come out in Hebden Bridge and the main street is converted into a *Biergarten* – a strange role for the heart of a town which, lying astride the Pennine Way, announces itself to motorists as 'The Pennine Centre'.

CHAPTER SIX

Bradford

Bradford is perhaps the most obviously cosmopolitan of West Yorkshire towns, the wool trade having attracted all sorts and conditions of men from all over the world to the city which has grown up at the *broad ford* of Bradford Beck. The beck itself is no longer to be seen, but it still flows underneath the city centre. There was a fulling mill on its banks by 1311, although in the Middle Ages Bradford was more famous for its shoes than for its cloth. When it did become well known in the textile field it was chiefly as a centre of the wool-combing branch of the trade. Even today it is in Bradford more than anywhere else that the long fibres are separated from the short by combing, the long ones or *tops* to be used to make worsted cloth, the short ones or *noils* for other types of cloth – tweed, jersey and rough woollens. The council run what is known as a conditioning house, where the weight and condition of wools, tops, noils and yarns can be scientifically ascertained and where consumers' complaints can be investigated.

But Bradford is also a worsted manufacturing town. The first large-scale spinning machine in the town, a mule, is said to have been installed in an old house in Barkerend Road, just above the cathedral, in 1794. The house, Paper Hall, is completely derelict, with a row of almost equally derelict shops in front of it, and a builder's yard at the rear. A notice says that it can only be entered with the permission of the local authority, and that, even when permission is given, the authority is not responsible for any accidents due to the house's dangerous condition. The fate of this building, dated 1643, is not at all untypical of what can happen to old houses in Bradford, a city which, till recently at any rate, has appeared to have little regard for its past.

It was not long after the mule had been installed in Paper Hall that Messrs Ramsbotham, Swaine and Murgatroyd built the first spinning mill in the town off Thornton Road, and it was powered by steam! By 1850 weaving had been factoryised and there were 129 mills. The population of the town had increased over 50 years from 13,000 to 103,000. More than half the Bradfordians were comers-in, and nearly 10,000 of them Irish, many of them refugees from the dreadful potato famine of the late 1840s. The Irish immigrants were virtually all working class, but there were some very important middle class newcomers: German merchants who saw Bradford worsted as a valuable commodity for marketing on the continent. The warehouse district in the Leeds Road area became known as Little Germany, but alas many of the impressive buildings put up there have been swept away, another example of Bradford's lack of concern for her history. The merchant families made an immensely valuable contribution to the commercial, political and cultural life of the town, one of the immigrants, Charles Semon from Dantzig, actually being elected mayor in 1864. Bradford Germans were largely instrumental in refounding the grammar school, which had fallen on hard times, and in founding the Chamber of Commerce, as well as cultural institutions like the *Liedertafel* and the *Schiller Verein*. There was contact with a similar colony in Manchester, and that city's orchestra, whose conductor-founder, Sir Charles Hallé, was himself German, found a second home, to which it still makes frequent visits, in the classical St George's Hall in Bridge Street. And among Bradford's most famous sons was a musical member of another immigrant family, Frederick Delius. Typically, his birthplace, Claremount, off Great Horton Road, has been demolished to make room for a garage.

Many of the German immigrants were Jews, and it was Charles Semon, along with Jacob Moser, who was to become Lord Mayor of the city in 1910, who founded the Bradford Synagogue. This small, chapel-like building, opened in 1881, is in Bowland Street. The design of the interior seems to suggest Spanish influence, which is something of a mystery since all the Jews connected with the life of the synagogue in its early days were from Germany and northern Europe. Among the most prized of its possessions is a scroll of the Law brought back by a member of the congregation from a business trip to Czechoslovakia. He found it in a warehouse, just one of a large number confiscated by the Nazis.

The contribution made by the German immigrants to the industrial life of Bradford was largely, though not entirely, on the commercial side; the major part of the production of textile goods was in the hands of born Yorkshiremen. One of these was Titus Salt, who, close to his mohair factory at Shipley, did on a larger scale what the Akroyds and the Crossleys were doing at Halifax, and created a new town for his workers. This was Saltaire, its name partly its founder's and partly that of the river on whose banks it was built. There is a statue of Salt, who was Bradford's M.P., in the city's Lister Park.

Lister Park was once the grounds of the house of another manufacturer, Samuel Cunliffe Lister, first lord Masham, who prospered through the invention of a superior wool-combing machine. His statue is in the park too, though his house has gone to make way for the town's art gallery, Cartwright Hall, named after the Rev. Edmund Cartwright, a Wakefield schoolmaster and the inventor of another machine which contributed much to the city's prosperity – the power loom. Lister's great Manningham Mills (surprisingly not a worsted, but a silk and velvet factory), still stand with their Italianate chimney over 250 feet tall, and the Lister coat-of-arms in bright colours over their Heaton Road gate.

Close to the mill is a large concentration of some of Bradford's most recent immigrants, the Pakistanis. While it seems a pity that there is not more integration with the native community, this area of the town certainly adds colour and character to the whole. The district's shopping centre, Lumb Lane, has shops providing goods of all descriptions so that a Pakistani housewife need never visit the city centre stores. Almost every building in the lane (known to Bradfordians as 'the Khyber

Pass') bears a sign in Urdu. One of the few that does not is the Conservative Club, but one or two city councillors have actually made an effort to learn the language so that they can converse with the people in their wards, while some of the immigrants have themselves put up for election. There are Urdu instructions in the telephone kiosks and on signs pointing to public lavatories, of which Bradford would appear to have painfully few. There is an office of the Muslim Commercial Bank in Lumb Lane, and round the corner in Marlborough Road, past the Corner Self Store (*sic*), which offers for sale both 'continental' (that is Pakistani) and West Indian foods, a branch of the United Kingdom Islamic Mission.

Marlborough Road leads down to Manningham Lane and the terraced but nonetheless opulent houses of the Victorian middle class. Away from town, in North Park Road for example, they are replaced by semi-detached and detached villas, while nearer the centre the houses are plainer but no less impressive. Particularly so is the recently cleaned ashlar terrace in Eldon Place which contains the Italian Consulate and a number of solicitors' offices. There are houses of a similar type in Little Horton Lane, on the opposite, southern side of the city centre, though some have shop fronts now. Some of the detached houses in this area (generally earlier than the houses in Manningham Lane) are splendid and in a variety of styles, though few are still private residences. One Gothic one is the university's Anglican chaplaincy; others are being sold off as development sites.

The University in Great Horton Road, which has West Riding-born Harold Wilson as its chancellor, is one of the country's newest but has its roots in the Technical College, built in 1880. A number of Bradford's institutions are Victorian in origin, and till recently the centre of Bradford was essentially Victorian in appearance. An attractive group of early Victorian buildings remains in the Manor Row area at the town end of Manningham Lane. Two of them, the Italianate County Court and the elegant Registry Office across the road display the royal arms in full colour. While other cities employed men with a national reputation like Barry,

Waterhouse, Street and Scott to design their chief buildings, many of those in Bradford were the creation of a local firm, Lockwood and Mawson. St George's Hall is theirs and so is the remarkable Wool Exchange in what was described at its opening as the Venetian Gothic style. This once world famous centre for the sale of wool and yarn is not the place it was though members still meet twice a week to do business and exchange news. The area around the Wool Exchange is full of fine buildings, made all the more attractive by their situation in a maze of streets on a hillside. The Midland Bank, built like the County Court in 1858 and also Italianate in style, is, like a number of neighbouring buildings, all the more impressive for having a corner site at the junction of several streets. It is a marvellous place with a balustraded top and Corinthian pilasters.

There is a lot of Italian influence in the buildings of Bradford. The best known is probably the City Hall, whose tower, again by Lockwood and Mawson, is said to be modelled on the campanile of the Palazzo Vecchio in Florence, although it also bears a resemblance to the tower of Siena town hall. The area around the City Hall has been made very attractive through demolition, the laying of lawns and the planting of trees. There is a fine view from the City Hall steps across the grass to the Prudential offices, bright red brick among the Bradford stonework. They were designed by Alfred Waterhouse, the architect of Manchester Town Hall, who created a similar building for the Prudential in Huddersfield. In both places his buildings have corner sites which helps to show off their attractive gables. He was less successful in his work for 'the Pru' in Leeds, where he was only filling in a gap in a row. Hard by Bradford's Prudential building is the equally good but modern office block of the Provincial Building Society. It walls in one side of a fine new square called The Tyrls, which was opened by the Queen on 13 November 1974. The other three sides are occupied by the City Hall, the new Court House and the Divisional Police Headquarters. The square contains a pool with a fountain spraying up from the middle of its waters, which are fed into it through what looks like a mock-up of a canal lock. By the side of the pool is a steel disk engraved with a map showing Bradford's twin towns. Part of The Tyrls has been set aside as a 'speakers' corner', and it is a very pleasant spot to while away an hour on a summer's day. There is one unfortunate thing about the square, however. The new police office cuts off the view of a very impressive group of buildings on rising ground to the south-west – the Odeon cinema with its green domes, the golden domed Alhambra theatre, and two big new buildings, an entertainments centre which includes an ice rink, and the city library. Between the theatre and the ice rink is a little garden with a statue of Queen Victoria from which there was once a grand view of the City Hall, but this is now largely obliterated by the least acceptable face of the police station. What a shame the city planners should have given and taken away like this. If only we could have had The Tyrls and yet kept the view.

The Library is one of the best of Bradford's new buildings and contains a good theatre. Less pleasing are the buildings which have grown up around Forster Square, the neighbour-hood of the city's two Victorian railway stations. Both are closed now, replaced by a new station in Bridge Street. The old Exchange station looks very forlorn. The 200-foot iron spans of its roof are still there, but the platforms have gone and so have the rails. There is just a vast open space, across which, looking equally forlorn, is the old railway hotel, the Victoria, another Italianate building by Lockwood and Mawson.

Forster Square is named after W. E. Forster, the M.P. for Bradford who introduced the bill for state education in 1870. His statue stands among the demolition sites. Just off Forster Square, behind the post office, is the cathedral; it was simply the parish church until 1919. Looked at uphill from the square it seems a dreadful hotchpotch of ancient and modern – a fifteenth-century church with twentieth-century additions to make it of cathedral size. Perhaps if the older parts were cleaned it would not look quite so bad. Indeed inside it is not unimpressive, yet one could wish they had left the old place alone. (You can see what it looked like before the alterations from the excellent model in the north choir aisle.) There are a number of fine Victorian churches in the city, most of them designed by Mallinson and Healey, a local firm who did for Bradford in the ecclesiastical field what Lockwood and Mawson did for it in the secular. Each successive year seems to see one of their churches disappear as hill-side slums give way to pleasant stretches of grass, but a number remain, St Mary's, Wyke, St Mark's, Low Moor, and big, impressive St Paul's, Manningham among them, But there is little doubt that the best is All Saints', Little Horton Green, a cruciform building with a polygonal apse and a commanding south-east tower and spire. What a grand cathedral this would have been for Bradford, and what a splendid cathedral close Little Horton Green would have made.

Little Horton Green is a quiet tree-shaded corner, like part of a country village, less than a mile from the heart of the city. It consists largely of seventeenth- and eighteenth-century houses and cottages. One mullion windowed house has a datestone of 1755 with the initials F. S. The S stands for Sharp, a family which included an eighteenth-century archbishop of York among its members. A particularly attractive house with two front gables is empty at the time of writing, and one hopes the same fate does not befall it as befell the two best houses on the Green, Horton Hall and Horton Old Hall, which were allowed to become derelict and were then cleared to make a hospital car park. (In fairness to Bradford council perhaps it ought to be said that their record where old houses are concerned is not entirely bad; they are maintaining eighteenth-century Tong Hall in another attractive old quarter of the city, and partly medieval Bolling Hall is one of the city's museums.)

Just up the road from the Green is Horton Moravian Church, a little bellcoted building with lancet windows, whose notice tells us that the Moravians began their work in Horton in 1741. They had other centres at Wyke, where their eighteenth-century chapel and adjoining minister's house survive, and at Fulneck on the Leeds boundary, a settlement named after the German town from which its founders came. Their Fulneck school has had at least two famous pupils – James Montgomery, the poet, and Richard Oastler, who is depicted with two factory children in a statue in Bradford's Nutter Place.

In 1812 a school was set up by the Wesleyans for the sons of ministers, three miles north of the city, at Woodhouse Grove, Apperley Bridge – a school whose pupils must have been among the first ever train-spotters. When the railway came in 1846 the school governors gave up some land to the railway company, who obligingly left a gap in the dividing wall so that the boys could watch the trains go by.

The boys were at one time examined in religious instruction by a young Irish clergyman from Hartshead. He was originally known as Patrick Brunty, but had lately changed his name to Brontë. (The popular hero of the day, Horatio Nelson, had the Spanish title Duke of Brontë.) While staying at the Grove, Patrick met the principal's cousin, Maria Branwell, whom he married in Guiseley church in December 1812. In 1815 he exchanged livings with the incumbent of Thornton, and it was at Thornton Vicarage, 74 Market Street, that his famous children, Charlotte, Patrick Branwell, Emily Jane and Anne were born. Charlotte was eventually to go to Upperwood House, Apperley Bridge as a governess (the preparatory school for Woodhouse Grove, Brontë House, stands on its site), but the place most associated with the Brontës is Haworth in the Worth Valley, where they moved in 1820, and their parsonage is a centre of pilgrimage, as indeed is the whole village. The church is often crowded with visitors, although only the tower remains of the building the Brontës knew. Their memorial tablet from the old church is there, though, and so is the certificate of Charlotte's marriage to her father's curate Arthur Nicholls, and the record of Emily's burial which Mr Nicholls entered in the register. Charlotte was married at the seventeenth-century altar which is now in the Brontë memorial chapel.

The Black Bull next door to the church, was one of the favourite haunts of Branwell Brontë and is much visited for that reason. One cannot get away from the Brontës in Haworth. The place is full of Brontë souvenir shops and Brontë tea shoppes, the proprietor of one of the latter claiming that it is visited by Emily's ghost on the anniversary of her death, though why she should want to do that is not clear; the couch on which she died is in the parsonage dining room. There are art galleries selling pictures of places associated with the family. One of the most popular scenes is High Withens, a moorland farm popularly believed to have been the original of Wuthering Heights, although the description of the house in the book does not tally. There is a Shirley Street and a street called Heathcliff from one of the main characters in *Wuthering Heights*. It is a pleasant place too – a group of houses with all mod. cons., built in the traditional way with walls of local stone and flagged roofs. Despite Brontë Ices and Brontë Tweed, an effort has been made to preserve the character of the town. The steep main street still has gas lamps and is paved with sets. In fact it looks like a northern town of 30 years ago and one can imagine being asked for one's ration book or clothing coupons in the shops. The feeling of nostalgia is increased by the sweet smell of steam from the locomotives of the Worth Valley Railway, perhaps the best known of all private railways in England. The company operates a regular daily service throughout the year, using diesel cars, and in the summer brings out one of its large collection of steam engines to pull the hundreds of tourists who swarm over the platform of Haworth station and clamber on to footplates in the sheds and yards nearby. The railway has been filmed by moving picture and television companies, *The Railway Children* being perhaps the best-known film made there. Oakworth station is still attractively decorated with the brightly coloured Edwardian tin advertisements put up by the film-makers.

The line leads to Keighley, a former municipal borough which included Haworth but which is now part of Bradford metropolitan district. At the northern end of the town are the beautiful grounds of Cliffe Castle, with fine views over Airedale. It is a lovely place to spend a summer's day. The garden is planted with rhododendrons and azaleas and children will delight in the attractively laid out little zoo of animals and birds. The castle, actually a Victorian millowner's house, is a splendid museum. There is a fascinating collection of the robes and insignia of friendly societies, including the uniforms of one lot who dressed like Robin Hood and his Merry Men, and a group of reconstructed workshops, among them the cottage of Tim Feather, reputedly England's last handloom weaver.

Another local record maker was the Airedale Heifer, commemorated in pub names locally as another famous beast, the Craven Heifer, is elsewhere in the county. The Airedale Heifer, which was killed in 1839, measured 11′ 10″ from its nose to the stump of its tail, was 10′ 6″ in girth, had 11″ of fat on its ribs, and weighed 41 stone. The heifer was bred on the East Riddlesden estate. The hall now belongs to the National Trust. It was built in 1648 for James Murgatroyd, a Halifax clothier, and has one of those rose windows which are characteristic of old houses around Halifax.

Up the road from Riddlesden is another seventeenth-century house, Kildwick Hall, which is now what is generally regarded as one of the best restaurants in the whole country. The same proprietors have another highly-rated restaurant in an eighteenth-century cottage, the Box Tree at Ilkley, which as well as being one of the best is probably one of the most expensive. From Ilkley, with its partly thirteenth-century church and its sixteenth-century Manor House museum, the A.65 follows the course of the Wharfe, towards Otley and the boundary with Leeds.

CHAPTER SEVEN

Leeds

Whether his first glimpse of it is from railway, inner ring-road or urban motorway, the impression a traveller must receive of the centre of Leeds is that here is a big Victorian city that is rapidly transforming itself into a city of the 1970s. If he comes from the south or west this impression is conveyed by St Bartholomew's church and Her Majesty's prison, which together make the hilly Armley district seem like a rather smutty Rhineland, and by the town hall clocktower dwarfed by new office blocks; if he arrives from the east, by other nineteenth-century churches, St Peter's perhaps, or St Mary's, overlooked by mushrooming blocks of flats. City Square, the busy heart of the town outside the station, strikes the same note. The station is quite new, and high above it rises the brick and concrete of City House, designed by John Poulson. To the north of the square are the sooty Victorian post office and equally sooty Unitarian chapel; in its centre the Black Prince is chief of a considerable group of Victorian statuary. But between post office and chapel, big and blue in the face, are the Norwich Union offices, apparently trying to make sure that even if Norwich remains a fine city, Leeds will not. To the right of them is Priestley House, another new building, named after Joseph Priestley, the discoverer of oxygen, who was once Unitarian minister here, and further to the right, beyond the chapel, Exchange House, 19 storeys high, but from this angle not altogether displeasing.

Yes, Leeds seems very much a city of the nineteenth and twentieth centuries, but looks are deceptive. Within the boundaries of the city, even before it became the largest metropolitan borough outside London, was a small village called Adel, and there the Romans had a camp. What is more, closer still to the centre of town, linking the districts of Roundhay and Moortown, is Street Lane, and since *strata* was the Latin term for a road and the Angles later applied their version of it, *straet*, to tracks used by the Romans, Street Lane is thought to have been a Roman road. After the Romans left, there was a district of the British kingdom of Elmet called *Loidis;* Bede mentions it in his history of the English people. It is though that the name meant 'the district on the river,' the river being the Aire, and that the district stretched from present-day Leeds eastwards to Ledston and Ledsham. Its administrative centre, and possibly, just before the Angles took over, the capital of the whole of Elmet, is considered by some historians to have been somewhere to the south of City Square, where there was, by the time of the Domesday Book, a manor house on the site of the Scarborough Hotel, and a mill, now commemorated in the street name Mill Hill, not far from where the Romans had forded the river.

Another separate settlement developed a short distance to the east – a church-town centred on a predecessor of the present parish church of St Peter, which may itself have been on the site of a hermit's cell. When the old church was being demolished in the 1830s, the architect of the new one, Dennis Chantrell, discovered in its walls some ancient carved stones, which he put together jig-saw fashion to find that they made a magnificent cross. For a long time the cross was an ornament in his garden at Rottingdean near Brighton, but eventually it came back to Leeds church, where it now stands in the south chapel. It probably dates from around the year 1000, and combines a representation of the legend of Wayland the smith with the figures of the Evangelists and abstract ornament. At Ledsham the church itself is still largely Anglo-Saxon, the tower being a Norman heightening of an Anglian porch. There is an Anglo-Saxon tower at Bardsey, and there are Norman ones at Bramham, Walton and Kippax. At Kippax the rest of the church is Norman too and made of what is known as herringbone masonry, alternate courses of stone laid diagonally and in opposing directions to make a zig-zag pattern up the face of the wall, but perhaps the most notable Norman building in the district, and perhaps in the whole of the West Riding is Adel church. The gabled south doorway of this little bellcoted building is sumptuously carved with Christ in majesty, the Lamb of God and the symbols of the four Evangelists, and the door still has its original bronze handle, the ring fixed in the head of a monster with a man in its mouth. There are no aisles and thus no fat Norman pillars, but there is intricate carving on the chancel arch – zig-zag patterns and animals' heads – and its capitals are carved with the baptism and crucifixion of Christ.

Adel church was built in the middle of the twelfth century. At the same time, those monks who had left Barnoldswick because of the climate and the hostility of the natives were building another church, Kirkstall Abbey. It is still there in Leeds 5, not far from the Abbey Bingo Hall and Abbey Home Brew and Winemaking Supplies. There are only two sides to the tower, heightened in the period when the Cistercians were becoming proud. The other two fell down in 1779, but the church is in a better condition than most monastic ruins. Its aisles are still vaulted, as are the three chapels on either side of the high altar, each with its own piscina or basin for washing the sacred vessels, and the west doorway, with five arches in one under a gable like Adel's, is really outstanding. Across the road from the church is the abbey gatehouse, to which the last abbot retired at the Dissolution and where he lived another 30 years; it is now an excellent museum. Admission to the abbey grounds is free, a good reason for forgiving the officials of Leeds council for not keeping the grass of the cloister cut to quite Department of the Environment standards. It was in the cloister that one of the most important archaeological discoveries on the abbey site was made – that of the monks' iron furnace or bloomery, the oldest relic we have of an industry still carried on at Kirkstall Forge, the oldest ironworks in the country, which now concentrates on the production of high-grade steel. An ancient quay was discovered at Kirkstall too, a quay from which, perhaps, some of the monks' wool went to market in the new town of Leeds, three miles downstream. This new town was created in a charter of 1207 by Maurice Paynel or Paganel, who held the manor of Leeds as tenant of the de Lacys, the owners of so much of the West Riding. It was largely built along one long street leading northwards from the river Aire, with the old village of Leeds on its left, and Leeds church-town (the present Kirkgate district, given by the Paynels to Holy Trinity Priory at York) to its right. The street was what is now Briggate, the city's principal shopping street, the bridge after which it was named being in existence at the latest by the year 1376. The burgesses of the new town were given their own plots of land in the district we now call Burmantofts (borough man's tofts), and were freemen, able to buy and sell land, deal in goods and administer their own justice. The lord's serfs still shared the big open fields which surrounded the old village, and grazed their cattle on the common which is now Woodhouse Moor, a public park since 1840.

Despite the development taking place in the town – a market well under way by 1258 and a fair established by 1322 – Leeds was still insignificant enough to be described as late as 1480 as being near Rothwell. Some indication of that town's former importance can be gained from the size of its Perpendicular parish church. Money was left for building its tower in 1460. There is another west tower of similar date at Thorner; it has the corbelled-out battlements typical of churches of that period in the Leeds area. At Whitkirk the church aisles have them too. Whitkirk is a pleasant village on the outskirts of the city which has lately been grasped by the tentacles of suburbia. Among the bungalows and the semis are several attractive old houses, notably the lovely manor house in Colton Road. In the same lane, on the east side of the church, is a little red-brick cottage with 1732 picked out in yellow on its green datestone. On the same stone is a double cross, a sign that it stands on land once owned by the Knights Templar, whose preceptory stood a few minutes walk away at Temple Newsam.

After the Templars' banishment, their Newsam estates, like

those at Temple Hirst, passed into the hands of the Darcys, and it was Thomas, the lord Darcy who was executed for his part in the Pilgrimage of Grace, who built the nucleus of the present Temple Newsam House. His crest can be seen sketched on the plaster in the Blue Damask Room in the centre block of the house. It was possibly put there as a guide to a Tudor craftsman who was to include it in some long-lost decoration. An original fireplace of Darcy's day is on the floor above in the so-called Tudor Room, although the panelling, bed and cupboard there came from Bretton Hall. On Darcy's attainder the estate was given by Henry VIII to his niece Margaret and her husband Matthew, earl of Lennox. Their son Henry, lord Darnley, who was born at Temple Newsam in the room named after him, was eventually to be the ill-fated second husband of Mary, Queen of Scots. Ludovick, duke of Lennox, a spendthrift, found himself forced to sell the estate in 1622 to Sir Arthur Ingram, who had amassed a huge fortune through usury and dealing in monopolies for the Crown. Sir Arthur's portrait hangs on the main staircase of the house, where he reconstructed the north and south wings. There is little sign of his work today; indeed to see the best interior of the period in the district one has to go to a church, St John's, Briggate. Ingram's work at Temple Newsam was 'modernized' by his descendant Henry, seventh lord Irwin, between 1738 and 1745, and he it was who turned the long gallery in the north wing into the saloon. Its beautifully moulded ceiling, richly carved door-cases, magnificent stone chimneypieces with overmantles in carved pine set with Italian architectural paintings, its gilt-framed mirrors on crimson walls, and original suite of chairs and settees with their floral upholstery, all help to make this one of the loveliest rooms in England.

In 1796 Frances Shepheard, the widow of lord Irwin's nephew Charles, rebuilt the south wing, an event commemorated by a stone on its outside wall. One of the ground-floor rooms is still hung with the beautiful Chinese wallpaper given to Frances by the Prince Regent; it is delightfully painted with birds, butterflies and flowering trees. This Chinese Room is furnished in appropriate style, the furnishings including some chairs in the pattern known as Chinese Chippendale. The Chinese theme is carried on into the Great Hall, where there are two incense burners in the shape of green monsters, like the lions from the Chinese ballet, on the refectory table. This hall was Jacobeanized by Mrs Meynell Ingram, who owned the house at the end of the last century and who had the eighteenth-century sash windows replaced by mullions. She also had the present main staircase constructed. Its design is based on a genuine Jacobean staircase that was once in Slaugham Place, Sussex, but is now in Lewes town hall, and it is one of two very fine staircases at Temple Newsam. The other, an elegant stone one with a fine wrought-iron balustrade from the time of the 1796 rebuilding, leads up to the display room on the top floor. It is one of the pleasantest rooms in the whole house, and full, at the time of writing, of exquisitely carved furniture, while the walls of the smaller room next door are hung with Eric Gill prints, for Temple Newsam is now a country house museum. It was sold by Mrs Meynell Ingram's nephew, the third lord Halifax, to Leeds corporation in 1922, and has since been beautifully maintained and filled with splendid paintings and furniture. The Ingram family portraits are still there, a number of them double ones of the squire and his lady, although the most impressive double portrait is not of a lord and lady Irwin but of Thomas Fermor, earl of Pomfret, and his countess, resplendent in their coronation robes. In one room, the Prince's Room, so called because Edward VII slept there as prince of Wales, the portraits are of members of the Savile family of Methley Hall. The door-cases and marble chimneypiece came from there too.

Methley Hall, a few miles south-east of Temple Newsam, was demolished in 1963. It had seen some stirring times, particularly during the Civil War when it was a refuge for Royalist sympathisers fleeing from Leeds after its capture by Tom Fairfax in January 1643; the vicar, Henry Robinson, swam the Aire on his horse to get there. Methley church is full of rich carving; grotesque heads hold up the chancel arch and stone angels support the braces of the roof. In the south chapel are the tombs of the Saviles, with John, the first earl of Mexborough, who died in 1778, elegantly reclining and pointing towards Heaven. It is said that childhood visits to Methley inspired the sculptor, Henry Moore to take up his profession.

Another church with some splendid monuments is Harewood church on the north side of the city. Among them is that of Sir William Gascoigne, the Chief Justice of Shakespeare's *Henry IV, Part II*. Harewood is a big church, yet there is no village in sight. The reason is that after Henry Lascelles bought Gawthorpe Hall, the old home of the Gascoignes, in 1738 with money made from the ribbon trade and collecting customs in Barbados, his son Edwin decided he wanted the church as a landmark in the park, but not the village. He therefore knocked the houses down and built new ones outside the gate. Edwin's village is a handsome one, built to the designs of John Carr, who also drew up plans for a new house to replace Gawthorpe, which was demolished. The interior of the new house was designed by Robert Adam, but some alterations were made by Sir Charles Barry in the 1840s. It was he who put the splendid curved mahogany bookcases into the library, one of the finest rooms in the house. He also made the plain classical exterior of the house look more elaborate, installing the Lascelles arms in the pediment of the north front, and removing the pediment on the south side altogether in order to raise the house a storey and provide extra, now unused, bedrooms. He gave that side of the house the look of an Italian palazzo, and added to its very impressive appearance by building massive terraces, with formal gardens and fountains, in front of it.

For older visitors to Harewood, which is now open to the public, one of its attractions must be its association with the late Princess Royal, who married Henry Lascelles, sixth earl of Harewood, in 1922. One of the most charming things connected with her is her dressing room with a domed fireplace alcove designed for her by Sir Herbert Baker and Sir Charles Wheeler. With its 'Adam revival' fireplace and window-like china cupboards, it resembles part of an oversize doll's house. In the Princess' sitting room are photographs of her family, including one of her brother, King George VI and his wife and children on his coronation day. But interesting as these and other relics are – and there are some really beautiful things at Harewood, like the magnificent Sèvres tea service given by the people of Paris to Queen Marie Antoinette – the visitor's eyes must always be drawn away from them and Chippendale's furniture, Rose's plasterwork and Angelica Kaufmann's decorative painting by the view from the windows. All around is magnificent parkland laid out by Capability Brown. The views are wide but there is not a factory chimney or indeed another house in sight, just open grassland, a lake (now with a splendid bird garden on its bank), and thousands upon thousands of trees. There are so many trees that it is hard to believe that 20,000 were destroyed by gales on two nights in February 1962.

The same gales destroyed 400 trees at Bramham Park, said to be one of the most remarkable examples in England of a park planned in the style of Louis XIV's famous gardener Le Nôtre. Here is not the artificially picturesque countryside of Capability Brown, but the formality of straight avenues flanked by high beech hedges leading to such eye-catchers as a vase on a pedestal, an obelisk or a temple. The house in the park was built, possibly to his own design, by the first lord Bingley, a self-made man who became lord mayor of York and Queen Anne's lord chamberlain. In the house is a portrait of the queen by Sir Godfrey Kneller, which she gave to Bingley. The best surviving statue of Anne is in the entrance hall of the Leeds City Art Gallery. (The city's many art treasures are shared between the gallery, Temple Newsam, and Lotherton Hall near Aberford, a Victorian house given to Leeds by Sir Alvary and Lady Gascoigne.) The statue was made in 1712 for the façade of the Moot Hall which once stood in the middle of Briggate. Briggate was the market place of eighteenth-century Leeds. Cloth was sold, however, in a Cloth Hall in Kirkgate. This was eventually replaced by two halls, one for white cloth and the other for coloured. The remains of the White Cloth Hall of 1775 can still be seen in Crown Street; just one front with an open cupola and painted green, it is now the warehouse of a firm of plumbers' merchants, a fact advertised all over its gateway in huge letters. On its north side, more tastefully painted, are the former Assembly Rooms, the resort of Leeds' fashionable society in Hanoverian times. Since 1815, the year of Wellington's victory, they have been known as Waterloo House and have been the warehouse of L. Hirst and Son, Tobacco Factors. The coloured cloth hall stood on the site of the present post office in City Square. Here was the fashionable residential quarter of Leeds in the late eighteenth century, linked to Briggate by Boar Lane, where in 1722 had been built the elegant church of the Holy Trinity. The new houses of west Leeds were built on the parkland of the manor house, and they were built of brick, for stone was a little less readily available in a largely low-lying place like Leeds than further west in the Pennine towns. There are still a few Georgian houses left in Park Place, but if you want to see them, hurry before they vanish or are altered out of all recognition. The ground floor of No. 6, which has a splendid five-bay pediment, has been spoiled by having big new windows put in, but the nearby offices of the Sun Alliance and London Group of insurance companies set a splendid example in tasteful restoration. A stone's throw away is Park Square, its gardens a riot of colour, still lined on three sides by eighteenth-century houses, now mostly offices. On the south side, where St Paul's church, which was built in 1793, used to stand, are the neo-Georgian headquarters of the Yorkshire River Authority. Next door is an amazing Victorian warehouse in the Moorish style which is at present being extensively altered to provide luxury office accommodation.

The rich Leeds middle class began to leave Park Square soon after it was built because of the smoke from Bean Ing, the city's first woollen mill. The mill in nearby Wellington Street has recently been demolished, but another factory belonging to the same owner, Benjamin Gott, in Armley is being converted into an industrial museum, a fate it shares with Moorside Mill in the Eccleshill district of Bradford. The well-to-do moved gradually up the hill to the north of the town centre. Just beyond the Merrion shopping centre is another residential development of the late eighteenth and early nineteenth century – Queen Square, its buildings partly demolished, partly dilapidated and partly taken over by the Polytechnic, its key park surrounded by wire netting instead of iron railings, but still, thanks to its trees and gas lamps, with plenty of character. And on its west side there is a hopeful sign – four renovated houses with doors of bright purple, red, yellow and blue.

There is another attractive quarter with good houses of the same period near the infirmary. The old infirmary, which stood near what is now Infirmary Street, just off City Square, was opened in 1771. The present infirmary, brick-built in 1868 to the Gothic designs of Sir George Gilbert Scott, is in Great George Street. Next door is St George's church, a building of the 1830s which has lately lost its spire and looks a bit odd. It has a nice six-sided apse though, and is built on a crypt larger than itself, a well-known refuge for down-and-outs. From St George's, a nicely arched footway leads over the ring-road to the cherry blossom of Woodhouse Square with its 1830s terraces and its statue of Sir Peter Fairbairn, a former mayor, who entertained Queen Victoria in his house when she came to open the town hall and was knighted at the opening ceremony. From Woodhouse Square, Denison Road leads to Hanover Square which has rather undistinguished late Victorian terraces on two sides, an older terrace on a third side, and the very grand and stone-built Denison Hall of 1786 on the fourth, its garlanded pediment topped by three urns. There are more handsome brick terraces opposite the University in Woodhouse Lane, and then come the grand villas of the Victorian middle class in leafy Headingley. Today the chief concentration of the wealthy Leeds middle class is further north still, near where Scott Hall Road meets Harrogate Road, and here, where some very tasteful and, for this day and age, very grand new houses are still going up, the tradition of lawns and trees established in the Park Square area 200 years ago is still continued.

Probably very few if any of the inhabitants of the rich northern suburbs of Roundhay, Alwoodley and Moortown have any connection with the people who moved on to the Park estate in the 1770s. Indeed many of them are descendants of immigrants

22. Sheffield Cathedral from the south-west, showing the new porch.

who arrived in the city less than a hundred years ago – Jews from eastern Europe. Unlike the Bradford Jewry these were not already well-established middle class families, but poor people fleeing from harsh treatment in Russia and Poland following the assassination of the reforming czar Alexander II. They had no connection with this event; they were merely a convenient scapegoat. The synagogues the newcomers built were named after the places they came from – the Marienpol, the Vilna, the Polish, and the Lithuanian. They were not the first Jews in the city, for as early as 1840 there was a Jewish cemetery in Geldard Road. Although it is on a cramped site, wedged between a railway embankment and a dusty main road, a long way from the main Jewish settlements of the last century and this, it is still retained, its vast crowd of headstones testimony to the Jewish feeling of community. The post-pogrom Jews settled first in the Leylands, just north-east of the city centre, but as that squalid area was cleared to make way for a new road in the early 1900s, they moved up the Meanwood Valley to North Street and them to Chapeltown, an area bounded by Harrogate Road, Roundhay Road and Harehills Lane. Today that area is largely occupied by West Indian immigrants, for sheer hard work the Jews, of whom Leeds has the third biggest community in the country, have reached the breezy heights of Alwoodley.

One of the most notable examples of Jewish enterprise is provided by the story of Michael Marks, who in 1884 set up in Leeds Market the Penny Bazaar that was the forerunner of the Marks and Spencer stores. Many of the Jewish immigrants worked as tailors. Some worked on their own in their Leylands' houses or in the crowded courts off Briggate, where one still comes across workshops like those of 'Maurice Feldman High Grade Tailor and Trouser Expert' and 'E. Rosenhead Tailor Alterations a Speciality', and others were employed by someone new on the industrial scene – the ready-made clothier. In 1855 one John Barran had set up a factory for the mass production of men's clothes; the success of his enterprise was due to three things – the newly invented Singer sewing machine, Greenwood and Batley's band knife which enabled cloth to be

23. Tickhill church.

cut in bulk, and, after 1881, immigrant Jewish labour. Barron's factory, which looks rather like a workhouse, is in that attractive area of the city centre near the infirmary. By 1900 some of the Leeds clothing manufacturers had started to retail their products themselves, notably Hepworths, whose impressive new buildings now flank the inner ring road, and in 1921 another nationally known Jewish immigrant, Montague Burton, began to mass produce off-the-peg suits in his factory in Hudson Road.

Today, tailoring is perhaps the best-known Leeds industry. In the early nineteenth century other industries began to develop on the south side of the river Aire, where the production of pottery was already well-established. (There is a fine collection of Leeds creamware at Temple Newsam.) The villages of hunslet, where only the odd pedimented house remains to remind us that this almost became another prosperous middle-class suburb like Headingley, and Holbeck, where the only memorial of the former spa is the name Bath Street on a wall by a piece of waste ground, quickly became swamped with smoke-belching factories and back-to-back houses. Many of these have gone now, leaving a depressing landscape of derelicton; but among the tips and partially demolished buildings are some of the most impressive pieces of industrial archaeology in the country. On Water Lane, where the only bit of welcome greenery to brighten the drab greyness is along the banks of the revitalized Leeds and Liverpool canal, is the chimney of Tower Works, a red-brick copy of Giotto's marble campanile in Florence, the white tiled walls of the boiler house at its base decorated with medallion portraits of famous textile engineers.

One of the major branches of the textile industry in nineteenth-century Leeds was linen production. Off Water Lane, in Marshall Street, is an amazing building modelled on an Egyptian temple, and known indeed as Temple Mills. It was opened in 1840 as a flax spinning mill and had a chimney shaped like Cleopatra's Needle. Its owner was John Marshall, who provided his workmen with a school and a library, and had grass sown on the roof of the mill in eight inches of soil on top of coal-tar mixed with lime, the intention apparently being to secure an equable temperature for the weaving shed below and at the same time stop moisture seeping through. There is a story that sheep grazed there until one of them fell through a roof light into a machine. Previously Marshall had had a factory at Adel, where he had employed a young man from Stockton called Matthew Murray to maintain his machinery. Later Murray went into partnership in an engineering business, and one of the things he built was locomotives. That was in 1812, and even today you can have a *steam* locomotive made to your own specifications in Hunslet. The locomotives Murray built were for the nearby Middleton Colliery, to take coal from the pit to town. The Middleton Colliery railway was the first in the country to be authorised by act of Parliament. That was in 1758 and the trucks were pulled by horses, but it was also the first railway to be operated by steam when Murray built his engines to run on a rack rail invented by colliery agent John Blenkinsop. The rack rail was abandoned in 1835 and the route changed slightly in 1875, but today the line attracts hundreds of visitors both for its historical connections and because it is still worked by steam locomotives. Run by a trust company, on weekdays it carries freight to and from local factories, but at the weekends passengers are carried in coal truck or guard's van on an exciting trip among the slag heaps. The locomotives are kept in the yard of Clayton's works; one of them is an engine of Danish State Railways with a chimney wide enough for a stork to nest in. Matthew Murray is commemorated by a plaque in Water Lane, not far from the site of his Round Foundry, and his iron monument, cast in the foundry, is in the churchyard of St Matthew's, Holbeck, a church designed by Dennis Chantrell.

Chantrell's best known building is probably Leeds parish church, a church with a very important place in English church history. It was built in the 1830s at a time when there was growing enthusiasm for the Gothic styles of the Middle Ages, and when the Oxford Movement, which laid emphasis on the Church of England's continuity with the medieval Catholic Church, had just got under way, and its architecture and services reflected these trends. It was perhaps the first parish church in England to have the surpliced choir almost obligatory in the Anglican Church today, and, with new emphasis on the sacraments, the altar, at the top of a flight of nine steps, was given the prominence that the pulpit had been given in eighteenth-century churches. Other post-medieval churches soon began to acquire choirs (i.e. spaces to accommodate choir stalls) and more impressive sanctuaries; Chantrell added a choir to his Lockwood church of 1829 in 1848. Leeds' sanctuary is magnificent. The marble and alabaster reredos contains three mosaic panels showing Christ in glory with saints worshipping on either side. The walls around are filled with life-size mosaic figures of the twelve apostles, St Paul and St Barnabas. St James the Great is dressed like a medieval pilgrim to his own shrine at Compostella, with the pilgrim badge of a cockleshell in his hat. Above the saints is a window of rich coloured glass, some of it collected on the continent and much older than the church. Another window in the south aisle was actually in the old Leeds church. It shows the church's patron, St Peter, looking very like the actor Hugh Griffith in one of his more Rabelaisian roles. The nave and chancel are filled with stalls and pews, and compared with the sanctuary are rather gloomy. On close inspection some of the 'woodwork', being in a Chantrell church, turns out to be iron. The organ is amazing. Its case obscures the pipes and includes three imitation church windows. Since the rebuilt church was opened in 1841 there have been daily choral services like those of a cathedral, and many of them have been broadcast in the B.B.C.'s 'Choral Evensong' series. When these daily services were introduced, the organist was the famous writer of hymn tunes S. S. Wesley.

Leeds parish church is rich in memorials, many of them to military men. One interesting and attractive monument is flanked by the statues of two infantry men of the Napoleonic period and commemorates Thomas Lloyd who commanded the Leeds Volunteers when a French invasion seemed possible. There is also something very rare among war memorials – one to parishioners who died in the Crimea, and a tablet commemorating the dead of the Leeds Pals Battalion of the West Yorkshire Regiment in the First World War. 1,200 civilians volunteered for service early in September 1914: fewer than twenty returned at the end of the war. There is a poppy wreath on the memorial with the poignant inscription, 'In Memory of our dear Pals.' Among the other monuments in the church is one to Richard Oastler, who was born in the parish but buried in the churchyard at Kirkstall.

Kirkstall church is another of Chantrell's. He built a number of churches around Leeds in the style of the Gothic revival, including Christ Church, Meadow Lane, which has cast-iron pillars, and St Peter's, Morley; but he also did a remarkable thing. More than 100 years after Christopher Wren's death, he gave Holy Trinity, Boar Lane the delightful Wren-style steeple which is one of the most attractive features of the Leeds skyline. One of the leaders of the Gothic revival movement among architects was Thomas Rickman. It was he who first classified medieval architecture as Early English, Decorated and Perpendicular, and he provided pattern books for other architects to use. St John's church at Oulton was designed by him; its fine spire can be seen from afar, rising above the trees in the parkland to the north-west of Methley.

A number of well-known nineteenth-century architects are represented by church buildings in Leeds. Gilbert Scott contributed All Souls', Blackman Lane, while the smooth light-coloured interior stonework, alabaster pulpit and iron choir-screen of St Michael's, Headingley betray it as the work of John Loughborough Pearson, designer of Truro Cathedral and of that most beautiful of English churches, St Stephen's, Bournemouth. Yet St Michael's is Pearson on an off-day. There are none of the mysterious vistas one associates with the architect and the view up the nave is too heavily punctuated by the arches carrying the roof beams. Surprisingly, much more satisfying is St Chad's, just up the road in Far Headingley, designed by the amateur architect Sir Edmund Beckett, lord Grimthorpe. Grimthorpe was a highly successful barrister who dabbled in horology (he designed the mechanism of Big Ben), and who provided a tremendous amount of money for the building and restoration of churches, which he felt gave him the right to interfere with their architects' work. The tower and spire of St Chad's make a fine landmark, but the church is all the more impressive because it is approached through an avenue of trees across a broad green. Perhaps the most impressive sanctuary in Leeds is in St Aidan's, Roundhay Road, a vast brick church like an Italian basilica, where, behind the altar, the story of its patron saint is told in mosaics by Sir Frank Brangwyn who also designed the famous ones in Swansea Guildhall. On the low screen between nave and chancel is a procession of people eager to receive baptism at Aidan's hands.

Although the Gothic style predominates in the nineteenth-century Anglican churches in Leeds, it was slow to be adopted by the nonconformists, who tended to emphasize preaching rather than the sacraments and who associated the style with a Catholicism which they regarded as something less than Christian. They clung on to the classical style until well into the century. The Brunswick Chapel near the city centre is classical; it was built in 1824–5. Outside is the invitation to,

Worship with us in this beautiful Georgian church . . . ONE OF THE MOST BEAUTIFUL INTERIORS AND ONE OF THE FINEST ORGANS IN THE NORTH OF ENGLAND.

The first Gothic nonconformist church in the city, and one of the first in England was the present Mill Hill Unitarian chapel in City Square, opened in 1848. The church was actually founded as a Presbyterian church as long ago as the reign of Charles II, following a Declaration of Indulgence allowing non-Anglicans freedom of worship. It was closed after a Parliamentary protest had resulted in the withdrawal of the Declaration, to be re-opened in the reign of Charles' successor, James, an overt Roman Catholic, who gave others religious freedom so that people of his own persuasion could enjoy it. There is an old radical Protestant tradition in the Leeds area, which was staunchly Puritan and anti-Royalist in the Civil War. At Bramhope is a Puritan chapel of 1649 with three-decker pulpit and box pews, while the church of St Mary-in-the-Wood at Morley is perhaps unique in being a United Reformed church which is a direct successor of the ancient parish church of the town. The old church, mentioned in Domesday, was let to the Independents, the forerunners of the Congregationalists, by the earl of Sussex in 1650 on a 500-year lease, so that while the Puritans' occupation of other English parish churches was only temporary during the time of the Commonwealth and Protectorate, here it was to be permanent. The present parish church is well out of town, while in almost every street there is a chapel with a name like Zoar, Zion, Rehoboth or Ebenezer. Many of them are used for things other than worship now, but they give the town an unusual atmosphere.

At Morley the Leeds-Manchester railway tunnels under the town, but there is an impressive distant view of mills and mill chimneys as the train approaches the station at the Leeds end of the tunnel. Among them is a very fine tower, that of the Town Hall. It was modelled on the Town Hall in Leeds, which was designed by Cuthbert Brodrick, a former apprentice of Lockwood and Mawson, who beat his old principals into second place in the competition to provide a design for it. Originally Leeds' city fathers did not want a tower; they simply wanted a concert hall better than St George's at Bradford, but built at a fairly low cost. Eventually they gave way to a pressure group which insisted that the building ought to be an impressive symbol of the prosperity and civic pride of the town and a tower was added, but it looks very ungainly. The whole affair is rather like a wedding cake. Both Morley's Town Hall and that at Bolton in Greater Manchester, which was also inspired by the one at Leeds, are more satisfactory. Brodrick was to go on to provide Leeds with other public buildings, all a little eccentric in plan. The most notable is probably the Corn Exchange, built in 1861 and an exercise in the use of the curve. A round building, it has a great elliptical dome for a roof, and arches (inside and out), porches and steps are all curved. It is one of a rapidly decreasing number of buildings from the late nineteenth century which till recently gave Leeds its distinct Victorian flavour. The Market in Vicar Lane was built in 1857,

149

but the exterior is in fact the product of a 1904 reconstruction. In what might be loosely termed an art nouveau style, it has clusters of towers which remind one of the sixteenth-century French châteaux of the Loire valley. A similar note is struck by the Metropole Hotel in King Street; but the market is built of stone and the hotel is brick, as indeed are a number of other public buildings including the old block of the University which was designed by Waterhouse. Brick of course could not be carved like stone and so decoration comes in the form of terracotta. A stone's throw from the Metropole in Park Place is the Irish Life office, a Georgian house which was given an amazing facing of terracotta flowers around 1895. Another similar material, but of various colours and not just orange-red, was faience, made locally in Burmantofts. It decorates some of the arcades, which, as in Halifax, are an important feature of the shopping centre. The Leeds arcades are glorious places, almost cathedral-like. Thornton's Arcade, built in Briggate in 1878, is a Gothic fantasy with a pointed glass vault and a clock with jacks in the form of life-size figures from *Ivanhoe* sharing the task of striking the hours.

Near the junction of the splendid art nouveau County and Cross Arcades, with their marble pilasters and gilded capitals, mosaic ceiling, and gates of flowing wrought iron, was once one of the most horrible slums in Leeds, Boot and Shoe Yard. No wonder Charles Dickens called Leeds 'a beastly place, one of the nastiest places I know'. Here on an eighth of an acre were 34 cottages in 1839, a density of 272 houses an acre, and an average of six permanent residents per room. From this yard 75 cartloads of excrement were removed in the time of a cholera epidemic. To see Dickensian Leeds – that is the working class Leeds of the writer's day – one now has to visit the streets of reconstructed houses and shops in the Kirkstall Abbey museum or search out the odd surviving yard like the gas-lit Crown Court off Crown Street in the now picturesque but run-down quarter at the bottom end of town near the Corn Exchange.

In the northern part of the city centre, not far from the Little London district where blocks of flats are rising on the site of the old slums, is the Merrion Centre, which has a new arcade: one of mock Victorian shops with fanlights over their doors, Venetian windows and mock antique signboards. There is a roofed-in square too and piped music. It all sounds horrible, but in fact it is a highly effective combination and the centre has a pleasant welcoming atmosphere so often absent from such places and even attracts Sunday afternoon window-shoppers. In it, or adjoining new buildings, are public houses, exotic restaurants, night clubs and a cinema.

One of the most attractive features of the Leeds of the 1970s is the large area of the centre which has been pedestrianized. What a pleasure it is to be able to walk the streets and admire, without fear of being knocked down, buildings like the gleaming white Leeds Library, opened here in 1808, the oldest subscription library in the country, and the Italianate Leek and Westbourne Building Society offices, built almost next door in 1852. But a threat looms over these pleasant nineteenth-century streets where concrete litter bins sprout flowers – the massive bulk of West Riding House, a huge office block. It appears to be leading an army of similar blocks across the city. Let us hope that their progress will be checked at Albion Street, which at present is the dividing line between the old and the new. Some of the best Georgian houses in the town have been lost to the developers and so has part of the Victorian commercial heart of the city, including banks and offices designed by Waterhouse, Lockwood and Mawson, and Gilbert Scott. Fortunately the Bank of England by Philip Hardwick, who designed the late lamented Euston Arch, has only been gutted for reconstruction within, and the old Midland Bank, a charming semi-circular building with a dome surrounded by a balustrade topped by urns and statuary, is to be preserved, probably as a public house. Built in 1899, it is very unusual for its date, and would not have been out of place in Regency London. It is undoubtedly the most pleasing building in City Square. May the enlightened counsels which have saved it also prevail in connection with the other remnants of the Victorian town round the corner in Boar Lane and Lower Briggate which are at present under threat, so that Leeds does not become so much a city of the '70s as to lose all its obvious physical links with its long past.

CHAPTER EIGHT

Wakefield

Leeds being the largest town in West Yorkshire, the city fathers assumed that it would become the capital of the new county and rented appropriate office accommodation, but they were wrong; the old West Riding capital, Wakefield, remained the county town after re-organization. Wakefield has much of the usual flavour of a county town and cathedral city. There are within the Wakefield Metropolitan District, however, two places which can rival it in historical interest – one on grounds of real antiquity, the other because of the important role it once had as the seat of the most powerful landowners in the West Riding, the de Lacys, and of their successors of the house of Lancaster. The first of these towns is Castleford, today probably best known for its Rugby League team and as a centre of the glass industry, but once an important station on the Roman road between Doncaster and Tadcaster where it crossed the river Aire. Scholars do not seem to be able to make up their minds whether it was called *Legiolium* or *Lagentium,* but, whatever its name, there are some interesting relics of Castleford's Roman past in the local museum, including fragments of pottery made locally and a milestone set up in A.D. 249.

The other town with a rich past is Pontefract, which again is better known for other things, particularly its liquorice sweets. Pontefract cakes were once made from liquorice grown locally, the sandy soil being particularly suitable, but now it is all imported. As was the case with Leeds, the centre of the town developed from three different settlements. The first was the pre-Conquest village of Kirkby in the neighbourhood of the

153

present All Saints' church, the 'church town' of the manor of Tanshelf. The second was the town which grew up just to the west of the rock on which Ilbert de Lacy built his castle high above Kirkby after receiving the manor from the Conqueror. It was a commercial centre providing for the needs of the lord's family and their retainers and guests, and its main street survives as Micklegate. This broad thoroughfare, which climbs uphill away from the castle, was where the market was held. Known nearer the town centre as Horsefair and Bridge Street, it shows no sign of antiquity now, having a bus station on one side and large blocks of flats on the other.

Perhaps in an effort to increase their revenue from tolls and rents, the de Lacys created a second borough to the west of the castle town in the middle of the thirteenth century. It was called West Cheap – *cheap* meaning market – and was indeed a very important and large market, the names of the streets reminding us of what was once sold or made in them. Even now on Saturdays several Pontefract streets contain market stalls, but the stallholders in Salter Row and Corn Market now seem to specialize in drapery and clothing. The broad Corn Market is a handsome street with a barber's-pole-striped butcher's shop at one end and the large stone Sessions House of 1825 with its Ionic portico and pediment at the other, and between them, on either side of the road, old buildings serving as shops and public houses. From Corn Market, the pedestrianized Shoe Market leads past a new and not unattractive library into Salter Row, a street which has unfortunately lost most of its character through demolition and the erection of very ordinary new buildings like the Argos Catalogue House showroom. It is at its best on market days when there are stalls down one side of it and colourful umbrellas over the tables outside the small two-storey, blue-washed Flying Horse on the other. In true market-town tradition, drinks are served in the pubs of Pontefract throughout the hours of market business. It certainly helps to make the town a very merry place, but perhaps it is also one reason why Saturday is the only day the parish church regularly suffers from vandalism. One or two streets in Pontefract (the name of the town means 'broken bridge', but no-one has been able to locate the bridge with certainty) still retain a great deal of character. One is Roper Gate, a pleasant avenue of eighteenth-century houses and shops which forms an attractive approach to the best street in town, Market Place. Market Place may be pedestrianized soon, and one hopes that the fine old buildings which line each side will be preserved and a halt made to re-development on the lines of the Woolworth store at its west end. If so it will make one of the best pedestrian precincts in Yorkshire, and give the stalls which cluster around the Butter Cross, a little eighteenth-century market hall, the opportunity to spread themselves all the way down the street to the fine Georgian Town Hall which blocks its eastern end. Most of the old buildings in the Market Place seem to be Georgian in origin, but Nos 33 and 35 with their overhanging second floor may be much older. Externally one of the most attractive buildings is the early eighteenth-century United Kingdom Hotel, though its disappointing interior is in the exceedingly plain 'modern' style of the 1950s. On the same side of the street is the parish church of St Giles. It too is eighteenth-century in appearance, its best feature being its tower of that period, with eight flying buttresses at the top forming what looks like a roofless dome. In fact the church is much older than it looks and the pillars on the north side of the nave date from West Cheap's earliest days. Pontefract was a garrison town, and its barracks now house the regimental museum of the King's Own Yorkshire Light Infantry. In St Giles' the roof is decorated with regimental badges and the two front pews on one side of the nave are marked 'Officers of the Garrison'. The mayor's pew, with a bracket to hold the mace, is relegated to third place.

St Giles' has only been the parish church since 1789. Before that, officially, the chief church of the town was All Saints'. It is a very curious place. It has a fine lantern tower, but, apart from its transepts, the rest of its medieval walls are a ruined shell. It was damaged by the Parliamentary forces during a Civil War siege when it was held as an out-work by the castle garrison, and for nearly 200 years just the south transept was maintained as a mortuary chapel. In 1838, however, Dennis Chantrell restored the tower and both transepts, and built a small apse at the beginning of the old chancel to hold the altar, and another one at the beginning of the nave to hold the organ gallery. The result was a church much broader than it was long, and in the 1960s a new brick nave was built inside the pillars of the medieval one, to make it more conventional in shape.

Pontefract castle is somewhat disappointing, yet it has been the setting for some remarkable events. Here in the Swillington Tower of his own house, Thomas of Lancaster was kept to await execution after his abortive rebellion against Edward II and his defeat at Boroughbridge in 1322. Here too Richard II died, probably of starvation and not in the violent way implied by Shakespeare, after the usurpation of Henry of Lancaster (King Henry IV), great-grandson of both Thomas and Edward, in 1399. The castle grounds, which, a notice tells us, are the 'property of Her Majesty the Queen in right of her Duchy of Lancaster' are now a public park, where, embowered by trees, we can see what is left of the castle keep. Near by, flanked by buttresses, is the twelfth-century postern gate, while on the other side of the inner bailey, which is now used as a tennis court and putting green, are the foundations of a little Norman chapel with a round-ended apse. On the edge of the green, converted into a flower garden, are the ruins of the castle kitchen with two big round ovens. With attention from the Department of the Environment and better labelling of remains, Pontefract Castle could be a much more interesting place to visit, although it would doubtless lose something of its picturesque aspect.

'Pontefract', said Dean Swift, is 'in all our histories'; Wakefield may have given the English speaking world one of the most written about characters in its literature. One of the supporters of Thomas of Lancaster proclaimed an outlaw after the earl's failure at Boroughbridge was a young man from his manor of Wakefield called Robert Hode, who lived in a house on the site of the present Bull Ring in the city's shopping centre, and who some historians believe to have been the original Robin Hood. What then of Nottingham and Richard the Lionheart? Well, there was almost continuous woodland from the Barnsdale area south of Pontefract to the Sherwood region of Nottinghamshire, and a fugitive from the law might travel great distances to evade capture. Indeed the same main road cut through both Barnsdale and Sherwood forests. And even the *Lytell Geste of Robin Hode*, a ballad published as early as 1495, mentions the Sheriff of Nottingham, but it does put Robin into the time of Edward II. It was not until 1521 that John Mair suggested he had lived in the reign of Richard I.

In Robin Hood's day, Wakefield was probably the biggest cloth-producing centre in the Riding and had other well-established trades too, and every year the craft guilds performed a cycle of mystery plays which has recently been translated into modern English. There is little left of the medieval town, however. All that would appear to survive is the chantry chapel on the old bridge over the Calder, where prayers were said for travellers in exchange for money to maintain the bridge, the bridge itself and the cathedral. The bridge and chapel as in the least attractive part of the city, close to an agricultural engineering works, a mineral water factory and a railway viaduct, and, although the chapel was built about 1350, its façade is twentieth-century mock-medieval. Kirkgate, the long street which leads up from the river to the town centre, has a mixture of very indifferent new and Victorian buildings on either side of it, one stretch in the form of a new shopping centre, bleak and open to the elements, with four tall blocks of flats incorporated into its design. To give them their due, the flats have an interesting shape, with every fourth floor recessed, and are not altogether a blot on Wakefield's fine skyline, though perhaps two neighbouring blocks are.

At the top of Kirkgate is the cathedral and here the city begins to acquire a new dignity, the rest of its centre having an undeniable quality. What re-development there has been, for example round the Bull Ring, has been on a very human scale and mostly in red brick, a material used extensively in Wakefield in the eighteenth century. The area around the cathedral, which, having been simply the parish church until 1888, has no close, has been converted into an attractive pedestrian precinct; and the cathedral itself has been cleaned. Its crocketted spire is 247 feet high, the highest in Yorkshire, a Victorian replacement for one built in 1420. The outside of the nave looks to be of fifteenth-century date, although this again was restored by Sir Gilbert Scott just over a hundred years ago. Inside, the pillars and arches represent different stages of building and rebuilding between 1150 and 1320, while the chancel was reconstructed between 1450 and 1475. Beyond a brass plate in the floor marking the site of the old high altar is a new sanctuary and chapel, added by F. L. Pearson, the son of J. L., in 1904. This addition is in the Perpendicular style and is reminiscent of King's College chapel, Cambridge and St George's, Windsor. It does not jar with the rest of the building in the same way that the extensions at Bradford do, and Wakefield's church is much the more 'cathedral-like' of the two. Inside, the feature of the building which has the most impact is the splendidly carved chancel screen of 1635, topped by a rood designed by the famous church furnisher, Sir Ninian Comper. On either side of the figure of Christ on the cross are six-winged seraphs who look rather uncomfortable, as though they did not know what to do with four of their golden wings. Beyond the screen are the fifteenth-century choir stalls. Among the carvings beneath their seats are a pelican, a Tudor rose and a juggler with his head between his legs. There is more fine carving on the monuments in the church. In the south choir aisle is Sir Lyon Pilkington, who died in 1714, in a marvellously curled full-bottomed wig. Near by is the recumbent figure of the first bishop of Wakefield, William Walsham How, the author of the well-known and well-loved hymn *For all the saints*.

If there is little of the Middle Ages visible in Wakefield, it, like Pontefract, nevertheless saw some stirring events in medieval times. On Wakefield Green, on the south side of the river, in 1460 the duke of York's forces were defeated by the Lancastrians led by Henry VI's queen, Margaret. The duke was killed and his head sent to York to adorn the gate called Micklegate Bar. His son, the earl of Rutland, was killed in Wakefield town when he was seeking shelter. The 'Butcher' Clifford has been credited by Shakespeare with his murder, but that has not been proved, although it is said that it was as a

24. & 25. *above: left* Dent Town; *right* St Giles' church and the market, Ponetract.
26.   *below* The monument on Stoodley Pike, in the millstone grit country of upper Calderdale.

result of his conduct at Wakefield that he earned his soubriquet. The Yorkists were, of course, soon to get their revenge at Towton and York's eldest son was to become King Edward IV. He gave money to the bridge chantry so that prayers might be said there for his father and all who fell at Wakefield. The duke's headquarters prior to the battle was Sandal Castle, two miles south of the city, where extensive excavations during the last ten years have revealed a considerable area of walling buried in what, before digging began, simply appeared to be a prominent bramble-grown mound. The moat has been dug out to a depth of 16 feet and six acres of the castle earthworks have been seeded with grass making Sandal one of the most attractive archaeological sites in the country.

Sandal's church of St Helen, although lengthened towards the west in the nineteenth century, is still substantially the one which the combatants at the battle of Wakefield saw. There are several other medieval churches on the outskirts of the city. The one at Crofton is said to have been built by Bishop Fleming of Lincoln who was born in the village and died in 1431. Another old church, at Kirkthorpe, is in a wooded setting and looks as if it should have a fairy tale witch's cottage as a neighbour; instead there is a group of sixteenth-century almshouses, while in the churchyard are the gravestones of some nuns who fled here from France at the time of the Revolution. A mile or two to the north of Kirkthorpe, is the big Perpendicular parish church of Normanton. Its windows contain many pieces of ancient stained glass, although none of them originally belonged to the church. They belonged to the collection of a nineteenth-century inhabitant of the parish who was himself a glass painter. The best piece is a fifteenth-century *Pietà* in the east window which appears to have been Flemish in origin. Another local church rich in old glass is the little church of St Michael and Our Lady at Wragby. Here most of the glass is Swiss, collected by the local squire during travels in Europe at the beginning of the last century, a time when no self-respecting young Englishman could return from the Grand Tour without a selection of another country's art treasures. Of the 19 windows in the church, 17 are filled with

27. & 28. *above* Pantiled houses at Boroughbridge; *below* Brontë country: the moors above Haworth.

489 panels or roundels of glass manufactured between 1514 and 1745. Apart from 600 panels in the Landes museum in Zurich, it is the largest collection of such glass in the world. The subjects include scenes from contemporary life, sports and warfare, as well as scriptural stories and incidents from the lives of the saints. In the top left-hand corner of the west window are William Tell and his son. The three middle lights of the east window, however, contain English glass dated 1534. The church itself is a year older, and on the chancel wall is the inscription in Latin:

> *Pray for the soul of Prior Alured, who had this*
> *choir built in the ninth year of his Priorate and*
> *in the year of our Lord 1533.*

Alured Comyn was the last but one prior of St Oswald's, Nostell, which stood close by, and in founding the church he may have intended providing himself with a living for the days after the impending dissolution of the monasteries. After the dissolution the priory estates passed through various hands until in 1654 they were bought by a London alderman called Rowland Winn. The Winns, who were already rich, grew richer on the profits of the mines on their new estate, where the monks had exploited the coal seams long before, and in time they were able to replace the converted remains of the old priory with a new house. Sir Rowland Winn, the fourth baronet, employed James Paine as his architect, but the fifth baronet, another Sir Rowland, got Robert Adam to decorate the interior and to add a north wing to Paine's main block. It was intended to build an additional wing on the south side, but this was postponed during the building of the stables (now a motorbike museum) and finally abandoned after the fifth baronet's death, with the result that the priory has a rather lopsided appearance. The house, which still contains many of its original furnishings provided by Chippendale, a son of the West Riding from Otley, now belongs to the National Trust.

Just outside Wakefield on Heath Common, within sight of a power station and the pit-head gear of a colliery, is a group of old houses which have been saved through the efforts of the Oddie family who live in the eighteenth-century Heath Hall. Unfortunately the Old Hall, completed in 1595, has gone, but Heath House, one of Paine's first houses, is still there and so is the Dower House of the same period, and the Priest's House, a sixteenth-century cottage. The school, which served the village for over 200 years, is the latest of six buildings on the Common to be restored. The 35-roomed Hall, which is open to the public, is a splendid house built in 1707, with wings added in 1753 by John Carr, known as Carr of York but in fact a native of Horbury just to the west of Wakefield. In that village is a grand town church with a Wren-type tower which Carr not only designed but paid for, and which became his burial place.

St Peter's, Horbury is not the only fine eighteenth-century church in the Wakefield district. Another, almost equally grand, is St John's in the middle of Georgian St John's Square near the city centre. Inside it is reminiscent of one of the restored bombed churches in the City of London, and the east end is indeed a twentieth-century addition in harmony with the nave of the 1790s.

Perhaps the most charming of the large number of eighteenth-century buildings in Wakefield is the little Unitarian chapel next door to the station in Westgate. It is built of brick like the big detached Georgian merchants' houses round about it. A feature of these houses is a recessed blank arch in the middle of the upper storey, a local architectural quirk to be seen not only in Wakefield, where the best house of this type is probably a motor-car showroom in Westgate called Austin House, but also in Pontefract, where there is a splendid example in Barclay's Bank in the Market Place. Wakefield is a very good place for a stroll of discovery – although it is more liberally sprayed with graffiti than most towns in the Riding – because it is full of nice architectural surprises. Most of them date from the eighteenth and nineteenth centuries, but a timber-framed house of the early seventeenth century survives in Silver Street. Well worth exploring is the labyrinth of courts, alleys and narrow streets behind this house in the triangle between Westgate and Wood Street. Here in Barstow Square, which is little more than an alleyway, is a large and impressive eighteenth-century block with pediment and blank arch, now used as solicitors' offices. King Street, the next street to the east, is worth walking down for a back view of some of the big civic buildings in Wood Street. The Inns of Court along here have what must be one of the best heraldic inn signs in the country. King Street leads into Burton Street, where the office of the West Riding coroner is a handsome early nineteenth-century stone house with Ionic columns on either side of its door. Round the corner is Wakefield Gaol, one of the country's top security prisons where most of the inmates are serving life sentences. Its new gateway with sliding wooden door and steel gate recently won a Civic Society award. From Burton Street it is but a short walk to St John's Square and a long eighteenth-century terrace called St John's North. Here and on the southern side of the city centre in South Parade, a terrace of about 1775 facing a green divided into gardens, are some attractive doorways and iron balconies. Perhaps the best eighteenth-century porch in the city is at 136 Westgate, where the frieze below its pediment is decorated, Adam-style, with urns and garlands. Number 95 Northgate has another prettily decorated doorway, and a little way beyond it, going away from the city centre, is the Gothic grammar school building of 1833. Its predecessor in Brook Street, built in 1598 and with the arms of Elizabeth I on its façade, has seen better days and is now used as a store by greengrocers from the neighbouring market.

The best street in Wakefield and perhaps the most monumental in the county is Wood Street. Here are the Museum, built as assembly rooms in 1820 and later used as a mechanics' institute, with two attractive bays in Crown Court at the back; the grand Court House of 1810 with its huge Doric portico and pediment bearing the Hanoverian royal arms and topped with a statue of Justice; and the tall towers of the City and County Halls, crowned with pyramid roof and dome respectively. Across the road from County Hall is Coronation Gardens, where, periodically, open-air art exhibitions are held. The buildings on this side of the street, police headquarters and health authority offices among them, are less memorable than those on the other, but Wood Street as a whole adds up to an imposing civic centre, well worthy of the county town of West Yorkshire.

CHAPTER NINE

Barnsley

One day in December 1974 an official car left the County Hall in Wakefield with some unusual passengers – three large plum cakes and a hunk of cheese; destination – Barnsley. 26 years before, County Alderman Lionel Cresswell had left £100 in his will so that his colleagues on the West Riding council and their successors could annually celebrate Christmas in the traditional Yorkshire manner. With the passing of the West Riding, the new West Yorkshire County Council not only maintained the custom but arranged for councillors on the South Yorkshire council, which now controls a large part of the old Riding, to enjoy it too (although owing to costs it is doubtful if they will do so again). Hence the strange journey to Barnsley, now the county town of South Yorkshire.

Barnsley was once known as 'bleak Barnsley' because of its exposed position, and it is certainly a windy spot. In time the epithet was changed to 'black Barnsley', and black it is too, less effort having been made here than elsewhere to clean up old buildings, even in the Victorian middle class district on the Huddersfield road, which has been designated a conservation area. It is black chiefly because it is the centre of the South Yorkshire coalfield, the largest worked field in England, and not only is it the headquarters of the county council but also of the National Union of Mineworkers. Although the district has a diversified industrial character and was once an important centre of linen production and wire-drawing, the monuments to the Industrial Revolution sought out by the industrial archaeologists are most often connected with mining. Before

166

the days of deep shafts and pit-head gear and for some time after too, coal was shovelled up from just beneath the surface or reached by short adits known as day-holes cut into the hillside. In 1838, during a terrific storm, the roads around the village of Silkstone were flooded and the waters rushed into a day-hole, drowning 26 children between the ages of 7 and 15 who were working there. A memorial obelisk commemorating the dead stands on the edge of Silkstone churchyard, close to the main A.628 Barnsley–Manchester road. The Silkstone catastrophe was just one of many such disasters which Barnsley people gradually learned to live with. On 12 December 1866, at Oaks Colliery at Ardsley, more than 300 men and boys perished in an explosion, and 20 or 30 volunteers searching for their missing comrades were killed by a second explosion on the following morning. The total number killed was 358. By the A.635 Barnsley to Doncaster road is an obelisk with a bronze angel carrying a wounded man – a tribute to,

Parkin Jeffcock and other heroes of rescue parties who lost their lives . . ., and also to commemorate the signal bravery of John Mammatt and Thomas Embleton, who rescued the sole survivor.

And accidents are still occurring, though mercifully on a smaller scale.

Explosions have always been difficult to prevent, but the invention of the steam engine, as well as increasing the demand for coal, did a lot to combat flooding. A walk through the busy colliery yard at Elsecar brings one face to face with an eighteenth-century engine house complete with beam engine for pumping up water from a pit. The original pit shaft is close by, and both are enclosed by an iron fence on which there is a notice warning the visitor of the possibility of explosions and of falling down the shaft. But the Coal Board officials are courteous to visitors and it is possible to see inside the engine house if one asks at the lodge.

The eye of the visitor to this old industrial site cannot help being distracted by a perfect example of an early nineteenth-century Gothic church with a beautiful spire – Holy Trinity – which stands on a hillside to the north. It is particularly noticeable because, unlike so much around it, its cream stonework is relatively clean. In the centre of Barnsley only Regent Street shows much sign of having been cleaned up. Regent Street is easily the best street in town, leading uphill from station to town hall. At the foot of the hill, on one corner is the town's leading hotel, the Queen's, and on the other the Regent Court Ballroom. This was once the booking office of the Court House Station, and before that, for ten years from 1861 to 1871, actually was a court, a fact witnessed to by the mutilated royal arms over its door; further up the street is the building which replaced it. On either side of the street are some pleasant early nineteenth-century houses, most of them offices, but a slightly jarring note is struck by two new office blocks – that of the Britannic Assurance Society, and, next door, the first temporary headquarters of the South Yorkshire County Council. Fortunately they are quite small and do not spoil the scale of the street. Bigger county offices have recently been opened further east as part of the new market complex.

Barnsley is no mere product of the Industrial Revolution. The town received its market charter from King Henry III in 1249. It used to have an open market, the largest in the north of England, part of it spreading up Market Hill, a broad street at right angles to Regent Street, to the neo-Georgian town hall with its Portland stone tower of a sort no true Georgian building would ever have had. The market was a picturesque sight which did a lot for Barnsley visually, but now most of it has been shoved into a dark and depressing market hall on several floors, with just the occasional hint of a lamented past like the Original Pie and Pea Stall, where one can get a pork pie in a basinful of peas for 14p.

Barnsley is another of those West Riding towns which unfortunately appears to care little for its past. Pitt Street, which used to contain the best collection of buildings in the place, is being torn apart. An ugly new post office stands at the beginning of the street where it starts to make its way uphill from Peel Square to Rickman's St George's church. A pretty little school building of 1813 has been replaced by a branch of the Y.M.C.A. with shops on its ground floor. The Temperance Hall, which was built in 1836, and the neighbouring Methodist church of 1846, both classical buildings with Ionic columns, are still there, and there are still one or two houses of the same period or even earlier, but they are in a pathetic state. Houses which would have been prized elsewhere have their windows boarded up and it seems to be only a matter of time before the demolition men move in. Yet just round the corner is St George's Road, a street of Victorian terraced houses which have been well maintained and modernized without losing their essential character. Nearly all of them, though still largely sooty, have the spick and span, 'little palace' look one associates with the house-proud mining communities. It is to be hoped that well-meaning but misguided local government officers never declare these houses redundant and destroy the sense of belonging to a community which is still felt in town streets and yet seems absent from the estates of semis and high-rise flats. But even here, round a bend in the road, are one or two ominously boarded windows.

Not far from St George's Road is Locke Park, given to the town in 1861 by the widow of Joseph Locke, a local man who was apprenticed to George Stephenson and in his day was a well-known railway engineer. This area, known as Kingstone, is dominated by St Edward's church, a big cruciform building with a central tower and as important a feature in the Barnsley skyline as is St Bartholomew's, Armley in the skyline of Leeds. It was founded by Edward George Lancaster of Keresforth Hall, who is said to have made a fortune from dealing in land. He is commemorated by the splendid west window which depicts 'the ship of the Church' approaching the New Jerusalem. The ship is a medieval vessel with St George in the prow with two children, and Christ on His throne amidships, surrounded by a whole crew of saints. It is one of the finest windows of any period in the whole Riding and certainly makes the trek up from town to the church on the hill worthwhile. The foundation stone of St Edward's was laid in 1900 by Edward Lancaster's daughter Fanny Jane. Her father built the vicarage too, and an inscription at the foot of the church war memorial tells us that it was used during the First World War as a convalescent home, 562 men receiving treatment there entirely at Mr Lancaster's expense.

Barnsley has a church by Temple Moore, the architect of St Wilfred's, Harrogate. Outside, brick-built St Peter's looks rather warehouse-like, but inside it is a spacious place with a high vaulted roof which looks like stone although apparently it is timber. There is a noticeable lack of stained glass; the windows have little diamond panes, rather dirty and broken in places, but one's eyes are drawn away from them by the colourful carving of the Nativity on the reredos and the statues of St Peter and St Paul on either side of the altar. The finest piece of furniture in the building is, however, undoubtedly the splendid Georgian pulpit.

The parish church of Barnsley is St Mary's, uphill from the town hall. It was designed by Rickman and consecrated by the archbishop of York on the same day in 1822 as St George's, Pitt Street. Although very much in need of a coat of paint inside, its shabbiness cannot hide its essential merit as one of the best church buildings of its period, and it has some interesting features. The Boer War memorial includes a most realistically carved rifle, sword, helmet and drum.

The church tower is Perpendicular and probably the only surviving relic of the medieval town. Even the medieval street plan has been partly obliterated by an attempt to build a new civic centre behind the town hall. Timber-framed houses have been pulled down in Shambles Street and an ancient barn has been destroyed to make room for nasty buildings regrettably typical of the new Barnsley – notably a big office block put up for the Department of Employment which looks out on to a shoddy square with uninviting concrete seats set among flower beds which support only weeds.

Poor Barnsley; a fine town has been virtually destroyed. One hopes that the few buildings of quality which remain will be rescued from the mania for destruction which seems to have afflicted the town planners, that the early Victorian houses in Peel Street and Dodworth Road will not go the way of their neighbours in Pitt Street, that the old grammar school building across the road from the parish church, and the Royal Hotel with the splendidly coloured royal arms on its gable do not disappear like a fine old house just up the street from them which housed the technical college annex.

One old inn which went long ago to make way for what is now the National Westminster Bank on Market Hill was the King's Head, the birthplace of the Barnsley chop. There are various versions of this, but the true Barnsley chop is actually two large succulent specimens fastened together with a skewer. You can still try the dish in the Brooklands restaurant at Dodworth, a former transport café which has acquired a national reputation among gourmets. Ask for a Barnsley chop there and you will find yourself confronted with what looks like a sizable joint of mutton.

Barnsley people have good appetites which are well catered for in the village inns round about the town. One popular spot is the Spencer Arms at Cawthorne; the oldest printed record of its existence is a notice of a sale of property held at the inn in a newspaper of 1788. The Spencers after whom it is named lived at Cannon Hall, a house built for them by John Carr which is today the property of Barnsley council. Here, at least, is one instance of Barnsley caring for something that is old, and very well cared for it is. As a country house museum it is less well furnished than Temple Newsam and much smaller, but the furniture it contains is of a superlative quality. Of the paintings, the best is something relatively unusual, a Constable portrait. We know his landscapes well, but it is doubtful if any are superior in quality to this splendid picture of a grey-haired, mob-capped old lady, Mrs Tudor. The first thing to catch the visitor's eye at Cannon Hall is, however, the splendid collection of silver in a case just inside the front door. There is also a room full of glass from many countries and centuries, glass having been made in the Barnsley district since the late seventeenth century.

Cannon Hall is in a delightful parkland setting characteristic of the west side of Barnsley. The view from the terrace over the lake is splendid, but just a little marred by new development, some of it in brick, on the edge of Cawthorne, an attractive, largely stone-built place which has been favourably compared with the best of the Cotswold villages. Prominent in the view is the tower of Cawthorne church. Although the church has some medieval work in it, it is largely the creation of G. F. Bodley, who was employed to restore it in the late nineteenth century. But there are some fine medieval churches in the Barnsley district, sometimes cropping-up within sight of slag-heaps and nineteenth-century industrial housing. A number of them were rebuilt in the Perpendicular style in the fifteenth century by a group of craftsmen who deserve recognition as being equal in stature, if not to nationally known Victorian church builders like Scott, Butterfield and Pearson, then at least to men with flourishing local practices like Mallinson and Healey at Bradford. Prominent among these workers were members of the Dayston family whose speciality was wood-carving. They are known to have provided the timber roof of the church at Almondbury in Kirklees, and there is similar work in the churches of South Yorkshire, including Silkstone. Silkstone church is extremely impressive, standing as it does in an open churchyard at a right-angled bend in a main road, just where it emerges from a shady stretch of woodland. It has buttresses all round its walls, with detached pinnacles connected to the wall by tiny flying buttresses, which are also a feature of Ecclesfield church in the Sheffield district. Inside, it is the woodwork which makes an immediate impact – tall box pews with the copper-plate engraved names of their original owners, and ornate Perpendicular screens cutting off chancels and chapels from the nave.

Among the other fine Perpendicular churches of the area, some of which are only Perpendicular on the outside and much earlier within, are Darton, Penistone and Royston. Tall-towered Darton church in its spacious green churchyard is a pleasant surprise among the factories and semi-detached houses just out of Barnsley on the Huddersfield road. Penistone's seems very much a town centre church, although Penistoma a quiet village till Cammel Lairds brought overspill industry from Sheffield last century and made it into a steel town. Even so it was busy on market days, when it served as the central stock market for a wide sheep-rearing area. It had a little cloth hall too, which still stands across the street from the church tower. Royston church is perhaps the most delightful of the group, simply because it has a pretty and unusual oriel window in the west wall of its tower. The local tradition is that it was put there to hold a beacon to guide the monks of Monk Bretton to the church. They owned the right to the tithes of Royston and had to make sure that it was served by a priest. They were responsible for the rebuilding of this church and of the chancel at Darton. The money they made from farming and iron smelting paid for it, so the Perpendicular churches of south Yorkshire reflect fifteenth-century monastic prosperity as well as that of the local woollen industry. The alterations at Silkstone were partly made at the cost of the parishioners and partly at the expense of another religious community, the monks of Pontefract Priory.

The original brethren of Monk Bretton came from Pontefract in 1154. The ruins of their new monastery are now in the care of the Department of the Environment. They are close to a roundabout where the A.628 Barnsley to Hemsworth road crosses the A.633 road from Wakefield to Wath-on-Dearne, and are overlooked by suburban housing. They are also overlooked by the people who live there. Ask the way to the Priory and you are more likely to be directed to a public house than to the ruins. It is a pity they are not better known, for one can spend a fascinating hour trying to reconstruct the scene as it must have been in the priory's heyday. The gatehouse with its porter's lodge is still very impressive, and so is the building from which the priory's estates were administered, its upper floor probably once serving as a manorial court. Only the foundations remain of the largely twelfth-century church. Some of the flagstones with which it was paved can still be seen and so can the tombs of the brethren, notably that of Brother Osbert de Gresby which has a clearly legible inscription. South of the church is the cloister with a book cupboard built into its walls, and on the east side of the cloister the parlour (from *parler*, the French 'to speak') where any necessary conversation took place, and the warming house where a communal fire was kept burning through the winter months. Then come the foundations of the guest house, and away to the east, isolated from the other buildings, those of the monks' infirmary where the sick and aged members of the convent lived under less rigorous conditions than their brethren in the cloister, some of them in private wards. Between warming house and guest house is the impressive main drain which once flowed with water diverted from the River Dearne. The water flushed away the waste from the reredorter or latrine block where seats were arranged over the drain. The splayed end of the shaft serving one of the seats can still be seen. The drain also ran beneath the kitchen. In a lobby on the kitchen's north side is a serving hatch into the refectory, whose tall wall with its fine big windows is one of the most memorable parts of the remains. The prior had his own hall in an impressive building on the west side of the cloisters. Here is a grand fireplace with a tapering stone hood, and another simpler fireplace in the wall of what was the floor above, although the actual floors have gone. When the monastery was dissolved it passed into the hands of the family of the earls of Shrewsbury, the Talbots, and they remodelled the prior's lodging for their own use, while Sir William Armyne, who married the heiress of the Talbots, built a new gatehouse adjoining this building, with the result that at Bretton we can now see monastic and secular buildings covering a period of 500 years from the twelfth to the seventeenth century.

One thing we cannot see is the monks' ironworks. It used to be in the area now appropriately known as Smithies, over a mile to the north-west, but its site has long since been built over. The monks of Rievaulx in North Yorkshire also had a smithy in the area, near Tankersley, but the site there was obliterated by the construction of the M.1. However, many medieval bell-pits can be seen from the motorway, and just to the west of it, in the woods, across the road from Rockley Abbey, is the furnace of an ironworks which was in production from the 1650s till the early years of the nineteenth century. Rockley Abbey was never a monastic establishment, but was originally Rockley Hall, the seat of the Rockley family. In the eighteenth century it passed to the earls of Strafford, who owned the next-door estate of Wentworth Castle, which itself is not really a castle but a very grand country house. Now in the process of becoming an adult education college, Wentworth Castle is not open to the public, but one or two of the follies with which its early owners embellished their estate can be seen from the road which skirts its grounds. One is an obelisk dedicated to Lady Mary Wortley Montagu, with an inscription referring to her introducing, in 1720, inoculation against smallpox, an idea she is said to have got from Turkey. The obelisk stands close to the lane leading to Rockley. And Rockley Abbey was itself one of the estate's follies, for Rockley Hall was deliberately allowed to decay until it looked like a ruined monastery. Now making the site look even more picturesque is a herd of Highland cattle, but the most interesting things at Rockley are the relics of its industrial past. The water of a nearby stream still runs ironstone brown, and at its side is a building which housed the engine used to pump water out of the pits. The iron produced at the furnace was apparently largely pig iron, a very impure and brittle form of the metal, and much of it was bought by a forge at Wortley for conversion into wrought iron. The huge hammers which did this work can still be seen, as can the reservoir which provided the water to power them. The hammers' wooden beam-like 'handles' have rotted and the waterwheels have lost their cladding, but the forge is slowly being restored to working order, thanks to a painstaking labour of love by the Sheffield Trades Historical Society.

CHAPTER TEN

Sheffield

Those who would seek to learn something of the history of a city or town they are visiting are often best advised to visit the cathedral or parish church. This is certainly the case in Sheffield where the cathedral has always been the parish church, having been given its lift in status as recently as 1913. On its site once stood a 9th-century Anglian cross which is now in the British Museum, though there is a picture of it in one of the cathedral's stained glass windows. Here too stood a Norman church, some of the stones of which are built into the wall of the fifteenth-century chancel, which, with an 'angel choir' in its roof, is one of the very few pieces of medieval architecture left in the city. The nave, although medieval in style, was rebuilt in the nineteenth century, and a new west end was added in the 1960s. Even though it looks something like a piece of Aztec architecture it blends reasonably well with the older parts of the church, and its towers, one over the entrance porch or narthex, the other a lantern over the extended nave, do not clash with the central tower and its crocketted spire, one of the most prominent features on the Sheffield skyline. There is however a slight difference in colour; smoke and fumes were so embedded in the older stonework that an attempt to clean it merely left it a lighter shade of grey. The western extensions were not part of the original plan to make the church more cathedral-like. Before the war it was intended to knock the nave down and to build a new church at right angles to and cutting across the ground plan of the existing one. Building stopped when the last war broke out, and the plan was later abandoned. But the foundations of the new nave are there under the grass of the churchyard, and what was intended to be the new chancel is now the military chapel of St George with an unusual screen of alternate swords and bayonets, a doubly appropriate memorial in this steel town. They were presented by the first battalion of the York and Lancaster Regiment on disbandment. Among the other twentieth-century additions to the cathedral is a suite of offices to the north of the chancel. This includes the chapter house, where we can see, told in glass, the story of Sheffield.

The first historical event commemorated in the chapter house glass is the building of a new church by Sheffield's Norman lord, William de Lovetot. He also built Sheffield Castle, which survived until the Civil War when, like so many other Royalist strongholds, it was demolished by a victorious Parliament. Its site is partly covered by the new Castle Market, and Castle Green and Castle Folds are now city centre streets. Other street names are echoes of a long gone, almost rural Sheffield. The Wicker is said to commemorate the wicker butts where the able-bodied men of the town practised their archery in order to be ready to serve their king in battle. Mill Lane, Pinfold Lane, Pea Croft and Well Meadow are self-explanatory. In Barker's Pool, the stainless steel flagpole which, along with the adjacent City Hall, is another very appropriate Sheffield war memorial, stands on the site of a real pool – Sheffield's first reservoir, constructed in the fifteenth century. Another significant street name is Burnt Tree Lane. It bears witness to an attack on the town in 1266 by John de Eyvill, a baron who had rebelled with the famous Simon de Montfort, earl of Leicester, against Henry III. The de Furnivals, who had inherited Sheffield through marriage with the de Lovetots, supported the king, with the result that castle and town were burnt, and the church had to be rebuilt. Another of the cathedral windows shows Wickwane, archbishop of York dedicating the reconstructed building. A roundel in the same window depicts Thomas de Furnival presenting, in 1297, a charter of rights and privileges to his tenants in Sheffield, freeing them, in exchange for payment, from their obligation to perform services for him, and giving them the right to collect rents which could be used for the good of the town. The Free Tenants or Town Burgesses of Sheffield remained the town's governing body right up to 1843, when it received a charter making it a municipal borough. In 1554 another administrative organization was created which still survives. In 1547, in the midst of the Reformation, the church's property had been confiscated by the Crown, but the papist queen Mary restored what had been lost, and in letters patent, which she is seen handing over in one of the windows, ordered that the property be administered by Capital Burgesses. Their successors still carry on their work, using the church's endowments for religious, educational and charitable purposes, and appointing the vicar of the parish, who is also the provost (or dean) of the cathedral.

By the sixteenth century, Sheffield had passed to the Talbot family. George Talbot, fourth earl of Shrewsbury, built a new house, Manor Lodge in Sheffield Park, to replace the draughty old castle as his chief Sheffield residence. There he entertained Cardinal Wolsey on his last journey from Cawood to his death at Leicester Abbey. George is buried in the Lady Chapel of the cathedral, which he built as his family chapel in 1520. On the other side of the altar is the tomb of another George Talbot, the sixth earl, who is today less well known than his wife Bess of Hardwick, but who deserves to be remembered as the gaoler of Mary, Queen of Scots, a costly and worrying occupation. Mary, a focus for Roman Catholic plots against her Protestant cousin Elizabeth, spent 15 years of her life (from 1569 to 1584) at then remote Sheffield, longer than she spent anywhere else. It is said that the Turret House near to Manor Lodge was built so she could watch the deer hunts in Sheffield Park. Little remains of the Lodge, which was neglected by the Howards, the dukes of Norfolk, who succeeded the Talbots as lords of Sheffield, and was partly dismantled in 1706, but the Turret House is virtually intact. One of the chapter house windows has a picture of Mary and her French secretary Pierre Rollet in the room there now known as Queen Mary's Room. Rollet died in Sheffield and his death is recorded in the cathedral register.

A house in Pond Hill near the city centre was once known as Mary, Queen of Scots' wash house, and there is a tradition that it was the lord of the manor's laundry. Today it is the Old Queen's Head inn. It is one of the few half-timbered buildings in the city.

Another Sheffield house which is associated in name with Mary Stuart is Queen's Tower off East Bank Road, not very far from Manor Lodge. Actually this house is only called after her and is in reality a Victorian building with embattled walls built in 1839 and enlarged in 1855 to form an occasional residence for the fifteenth duke of Norfolk. As lords of the manor, the dukes, although opposing anything detrimental to their own interests, played an important part in the development of the city in the eighteenth and nineteenth centuries. Roman Catholics themselves, one of them made available a room for Romanist worship in Fargate in 1767. Later, in 1815, a chapel was built in Norfolk Row, and the impressive church of St Marie replaced it in 1850, its fine spire rivalling that of the cathedral. Marie is no French saint but the mother of Jesus, the spelling of her name being a reflection of the absorbing interest in things medieval among upper class and intellectual Roman Catholics and High Anglicans in the middle of the last century.

One of the dukes built the mock-Tudor Shrewsbury Almhouses in Norfolk Road in 1825 to replace some nearer the town centre, and later lords of the manor donated a great deal of land for parks, helping to endow Sheffield with a larger acreage of parks, open woods and recreation grounds than any other English city.

It was a duke of Norfolk who was the city's first lord mayor. Sheffield's chief citizen was given the title by Queen Victoria following her visit in 1897, her Diamond Jubilee year, to open the city's new town hall. (Sheffield became a city in 1893, on the fiftieth anniversary of her incorporation as a borough.) The cupola of the elaborate town hall tower is topped by a massive statue of Vulcan, the blacksmith god and symbol of the city's dominant industry. You cannot get away from iron and steel in Sheffield city, although a large part of the metropolitan district outside the old city boundaries is open moorland.

The omnispresence of the industry is not surprising since the existence of an ancient forge at Wincobank suggests that iron may have been produced here in pre-Christian times. (The two-and-a-half-acre Wincobank Camp, on a spur above the Don valley, has been dated to the first century B.C.) And there were smithies in Sheffield Park in the thirteenth century. As one might expect, the industry is represented in the cathedral's chapter house windows. The most famous of the windows shows the Canterbury pilgrims en route to the shrine of St Thomas Becket. They are there because Chaucer wrote of the miller, 'A Sheffield thwitel baar he in his hose.' The thwitel was the meat knife carried by everyone for table use in the days before the provision of cutlery by hostesses. Knife blades were for centuries ground in water-powered workshops called hulls situated along the banks of Sheffield's five rivers – the Don and its tributaries, the Sheaf, the Loxley, the Rivelin and the Porter Brook. The Shepherd Wheel still survives on the banks of the Porter in Whitley woods, where it and its predecessors have driven grinding wheels since at least 1584, the date of the first known documentary mention of 'Porter Wheel'. Upstream is another important industrial site, that of Thomas Boulsover's rolling mill for producing Sheffield Plate. Wire Mill Dam, which held the water to drive its machinery, still survives, and nearby there is a memorial to Boulsover. The process which he invented in the 1740s involved melting silver and fusing it with a copper alloy so that the two metals could be rolled together. It meant that articles of many kinds which had previously been made out of silver could now be produced much less expensively and yet look just like genuine silverware. The Sheffield museum in Weston Park has the world's best collection of old Sheffield Plate. Electro-plating eventually came to be used to produce substitute silverware, and the manufacture of the much superior Sheffield Plate became a lost art. But a further important invention connected with the production of cutlery and tableware was to be made in Sheffield. This was stainless steel, discovered by a local lad, Harry Brearley, in 1913.

The simplest form of steel was blistered steel formed by the cementation process which involved adding carbon, in the form of charcoal, to heated iron bars. The oxygen in the iron would unite with the carbon to form carbon monoxide and the metal remaining would then be in a more or less pure state. The bars, which had acquired a blistered appearance, might then be sheared into small lengths and raised to welding heat in a furnace, after which they would be beaten under a tilt hammer till they combined into one rod with uniform tenacity and density throughout. A conical furnace for the production of this 'shear-steel' was recently discovered in Bower Spring and is being preserved as the earliest standing monument to the city's place as the steel centre of the world. At Abbeydale on the A.621 Sheffield to Bakewell road is a scythe works which operated at least from 1712 to 1933 and is now an industrial museum, where one can see the complete process of scythe manufacture, including the production of steel in a crucible furnace, the invention of a Sheffield clockmaker Benjamin Huntsman (another subject of the cathedral glass designer) about 1740. He wanted a really hard, good quality steel for clock springs and both blistered steel and shear-steel were unsuitable, so he heated both together in a clay crucible along with a flux of secret composition. The white-hot material was then teemed from the crucible into a mould, a hand operation requiring great skill, and one which is occasionally demonstrated at Abbeydale. Huntsman's own works at Attercliffe still survives though greatly enlarged. The newer steel mills lack the visual appeal of many of the textile mills for they are built not of stone but of their own products. They are vast, steel-framed, corrugated iron sheds with steel chimneys, and contrast greatly with little Abbeydale, which is stone-built and unusually attractive. Much of the water-powered machinery there can be seen working. The tilt forge was built in 1785 and the grinding shop in 1817. In addition to the workshops there is a row of late eighteenth-century workmen's cottages and the nineteenth-century manager's house with appropriate Victorian furnishings.

Sheffield has always prided itself on the high quality of its manufactures. At one time substandard products were publicly destroyed in Paradise Square by the Master Cutler, the elected head of the manufacturers' guild. The square is near the cathedral, a delightful close surrounded by elegant eighteenth-century brick houses which is all the more attractive for being partially cobbled and built on a slope. Here, in July 1779, John Wesley preached to 'the largest congregation I ever saw on a weekday'.

Uphill from Paradise Square, right opposite the cathedral, is the neo-classical bulk of the Cutlers' Hall. Here the Cutlers' feast takes place every year, and the well-heeled manufacturers sup on brewis, a traditional broth sprinkled with oatcake, once the staple diet of a Sheffield apprentice. The Cutlers' Company was founded in 1624, but even before that goods were being produced which bore the distinctive mark of a master cutler. William Elles is the first cutler known to have used a private mark. One of the cathedral windows shows him receiving permission to use it from a court held on 2 October 1554. Today the names of the Sheffield cutlers and their marks are well known throughout England and beyond. They forged their way up from the crowded houses and workshops crammed on to the gardens of the old burgesses' houses in the town to big suburban mansions in bracing Ranmoor. Their residences are still there but few of them are family houses now. Some are hotels and guest houses and the spacious gardens of others accommodate schools and university hostels. The house of Mark Firth, who made his mark not only in the steel industry but outside it as the founder of the college which became Sheffield University, is now the Convent of Notre Dame. Perhaps the most notable of these houses is Endcliffe Hall in Vale Road, the Italianate home of Sir John Brown, the first Sheffield ironmaster to use a new tool of steel manufacture, the Bessemer 'converter', in which iron could be turned into steel in half-an-hour instead of the previous 15 to 20 days. Bessemer, who thought of the process in 1856, later established his own factory next door to Sir John's in Brightside.

Coke provided the carbon element in the Bessemer process. Coal which could be converted into coke was mined locally, and the lords of the manor exploited the coal seams under Sheffield Park. No collieries are there now. At the city centre end of the old park area the scene is dominated by huge blocks of flats, high above the Don valley and the railway. The council estates of Sheffield, designed by the city architect J. L. Womersley, have been highly praised by architectural experts. The block of flats on Park Hill rises to 14 storeys in places, and every three storeys there is a ten-foot-wide deck for the milkman to drive along, for the children to play on and for housewives to gossip on. The intimacy of the old working class streets has in a sense been re-created, but when 2,000 dwellings are erected on a site once occupied by 800 do we also re-create potential slum conditions?

Another interesting development in Sheffield is Castle Square at the east end of the shopping centre. Here what is known as the 'hole in the road' combines a roundabout with a pedestrian underpass and a shopping precinct which has basement level access to a number of big stores and the market. There is a small garden in the middle of the 'hole' at the heart of the roundabout. The architects must have been James Bond fans, for their design incorporated a tank of very toothy piranha fish! Sheffield has a huge shopping centre from Castle Square up the pedestrianised precinct of High Street and Fargate to The Moor, a parade of big stores itself half-a-mile long, and the city has the biggest toy shop in Europe. Little wonder there are special buses on Saturdays bringing customers from Stoke-on-Trent and the Potteries to Yorkshire's largest shopping place, where there are more department stores than in any other city north of London. Round the outside of the shopping area is a new ring road, Arundel Gate, named after the old family seat of the dukes of Norfolk. This is being developed as the city's entertainment area. It includes the Crucible Theatre, the first full-scale theatre in the country to have a deep thrust or promontory stage with the audience seated on three sides, as well as the Fiesta, the biggest night club in Europe. Ambitious Sheffield does indeed appear to be what it claims, a 'city on the move'.

CHAPTER ELEVEN

Rotherham

Sheffield has been much criticised in the past for its dirt and its smoke. In the 1882 edition of *Murray's Handbook for Yorkshire* it was described as 'beyond all question the blackest, dirtiest and least agreeable' town in the county, and for many visitors its only redeeming feature was the easy access to the moors which surround it. There is a phrase much used of Sheffield which has been attributed both to Ruskin and to Palmerston – 'a dirty picture in a lovely frame' is one version of it – which for many people still sums up Sheffield. But the people who use it are probably not aware that Sheffield now claims to have the cleanest air of any industrial city in Europe, if not in the world. Those who travel on the M.1 over the Tinsley viaduct high above the river Don might not be inclined to agree, for all they can see is factory after factory overhung by a pall of smoke. True, from observation of the signposts some of them might think that none of this is Sheffield at all, but that it all belongs to neighbouring Rotherham – something which does not please Rotherham people who claim that Sheffield's city centre is only clean because the biggest steel works are on their side of the city and the prevailing winds bring them the smoke that rightfully is Sheffield's.

However, Rotherham does have its own steel works, particularly in the Masbrough area of the town, a depressing industrial suburb which is gradually being cleared of shoddy working class terraced houses. The council try to rebuild on the demolition sites so that people can stay with their friends and neighbours and there will be no unsightly pieces of waste ground in downtown areas. But there are some areas of newish housing further away from the centre, for example along the Wortley Road.

A little further up the same road (A.629) is one of the most remarkable industrial sites in the whole country – Kirkstead Abbey Grange. In May 1161 Richard de Busli, lord of the manor of Kimberworth, granted to the monks of Kirkstead Abbey in Lincolnshire,

> *a site for their houses and an orchard and four forges, to wit two for smelting iron and two for forging it, whensoever they wish, and leave to dig for ore throughout their territory (of Kimberworth), so much as would be sufficient for two furnaces and also enough deadwood of Kimberworth for the four furnaces.*

Hummocks on the hillside which slopes down from Thorpe Common to the Blackburn Brook betray the site of the monks' mine workings, and at the top of the hill, opposite the Sportsman inn, are the monks' smithy houses, restored in 1900 and still with their Norman windows, but now rather dilapidated.

The iron and steel industry was to bring both squalor and prosperity to the citizens of Rotherham. A family which owned one of the Masbrough iron works (where cannon were cast for the American Civil War), the Walkers, had a fine house in parkland on the east side of the town called Clifton House, built in 1782 to a design by John Carr. It is now Rotherham's museum, where just inside the front door one is greeted by Nelson, a South African lion who died, aged 25, in the zoological gardens, London in 1872. The Walker family portraits are still there, including an unusual one of a boy, a girl and a dog playing together. The frame at the foot of the elegant wrought-iron staircase which should contain the picture of Susannah, the wife of Joshua Walker, who died in 1831, is strangely empty, but the museum showcases are full of interesting exhibits. There is a fine collection of the locally produced Rockingham china. Just one kiln remains of the original pottery which had a comparatively brief life from 1745 to 1842.

This is the Waterloo Kiln, built in 1815, the year of the battle, which can be seen in the trees, across a field from the lane which leads from the roundabout on the A.633 at Swinton towards Upper Haugh. Also in Rotherham museum is the fine gravestone of a soldier of the first cohort of Gauls. There was a Roman fort covering six acres at Templeborough to the west of the town, but its site is now covered by a steel works. However, the colonnade and columns from the portico of the large granaries can be seen among the magnolias and buddleia trees in Clifton Park.

There is not much of any great age in Rotherham itself except for the odd survival like the fourteenth-century, timber-framed, former Three Cranes Inn in High Street which is now Wakefield's Army Stores, but it is a pleasant largely nineteenth- and early twentieth-century town with broad streets and little that looks out of place or out of scale. The new market hall, which holds a market granted by Edward I, itself the successor of one granted by King John, who also gave permission for the annual Statute Fair which is still held, is of a pleasing modern design but at the same time low and unobtrusive. And Beeversleigh, the town's first tower block of flats, a hexagonal building reinforced with a concrete 'cage' after London's Ronan Point disaster, may be its last, since Rotherham's housing problem has been largely solved. Of course, the huge power station is hardly an ornament to the town but it lies out of the way by the river. The water used in the production of electricity comes from Wellgate Spring, once the source of the town's own water supply and referred to as such in a document of 1549. In Wellgate is an unusual item of street furniture — an old lamp standard hidden in the hedge of number 1 Wellgate Terrace, the only surviving relic of the 135 oil lamps which lit the town before gas lighting was introduced in 1833. Rotherham has an number of ornate lamp standards, the most elaborate and gaudily coloured being those outside the otherwise undistinguished town hall.

One of the most notable buildings in the town is the Chapel on the Bridge. Neater, less elaborate and more attractive than the one in Wakefield, it was begun in 1483, the year John

Bokyng, grammar master at the local school, Jesus College, died and in his will left '3s 4d towards the fabric of the chapel to be built on Rotherham bridge'. It was dissolved in common with other non-parochial chapels and chantries by Edward VI's ultra-Protestant government in 1547, and its endowments were confiscated. It was later used as an almshouse, the town's prison, an isolation hospital in time of plague, and, from 1881 to 1913, as a tobacconist's shop. It was restored, given its very attractive new window tracery, and re-opened for worship in 1924.

From the old bridge one can see the finest of Rotherham's buildings, the grand Perpendicular parish church of rich red sandstone, with the spire of its central tower reaching 180 feet into the sky. The most impressive church in South Yorkshire, and perhaps, with the possible exceptions of Selby Abbey and Ripon Cathedral, in the whole of the West Riding, it stands on a rise high above the paved All Saints' Square with its fountains and coloured umbrellas. Judging from old prints, the graveyard on the other side of the building was little more than a walled piece of moorland at the beginning of the last century, but now it is an attractive tree-shaded close, from which one can admire the elaborate carving of the church's eighteenth-century restorers. The interior is quite majestic. The fine fan vaulting of the tower is considered by some architectural historians to be among the earliest in England, the building of the tower having been begun in 1409. The nave and chancel have wooden ceilings with carved bosses which date from 1450 and 1510 respectively. In the chancel the return stalls are decorated with fifteenth-century carved figures telling the story of the Nativity – the angels of the Annunciation, Mary kneeling to receive their news, the Wise Men with their gifts. and Mary and Joseph with the infant Jesus. The great east window of the Te Deum, designed by Sir Gilbert Scott, who also designed the reredos with its figures of saints, was taken out during the Second World War and put down a nearby coalmine for safe-keeping. It was given by the lord of the manor, the earl of Effingham, a kinsman of the Howards of Sheffield. Under the sanctuary carpet is a slab with a rare inscription:

Here is interred the bowels of Jane, Duchess of Norfolk 1693.

Her body was taken to the family vaults at Arundel. The most interesting family memorial in the church is in the north chapel – the sixteenth-century brass of Robert Swift with his wife and children. Next to it is the safe containing the church archives. The registers are among the oldest in England, dating back to 1540, and among the entries is a record of the marriage in 1844, of Anthony Trollope, author and inventor of pillar boxes, to Rose Heseltine, daughter of the manager of the bank which is now Williams and Glyn's on the corner of High Street and Wellgate. In the north transept of the church is the fine eighteenth-century organ case with gilded pipes; the recent rude extension of the organ in the adjoining choir vestry is just about the only thing which mars the appearance of this beautiful church.

The south chapel, known as the Jesus Chapel, was reputedly founded by Thomas Scott, who was born in 1423 on the site now occupied by Woolworth's stores and who later, having adopted the name of Rotherham, became bishop of Lincoln and Rochester, chancellor of Cambridge university, ambassador to France, chancellor of England and archbishop of York. He befriended Elizabeth Woodville, Edward IV's widow and mother of the Princes in the Tower, and was himself put in the Tower by Richard III. In his home town he founded Jesus College which stood near where Marks and Spencer's is now and appointed a provost and three fellows to teach grammar, writing, arithmetic and singing to local boys. Because it was a religious foundation the College was dissolved, like the chapel on the bridge, in 1547, but at the same time, as often happened in such a case, a new grammar school was founded by King Edward VI with the old college's endowments. It was the school's Old Boys Association which, in 1963, installed a stained glass window commemorating Thomas in the Jesus Chapel. Today, after comprehensivization the former buildings of the school, public school-like with their tower above a vast green playing field, house the Thomas Rotherham Sixth-Form College. The college is in a leafy middle class suburb, so different from Masbrough, on the south side of the town centre.

The Rotherham district is an area of contrasts. Everywhere there is lovely countryside cheek by jowl with factories and industrial waste. Not far from the centre of Rotherham itself, up a lane called The Green, off a busy main road, is the delightfully secluded green churchyard of Whiston, with the ivy-covered Norman tower of the church of St Mary Magdalene. A mile or two further south, not far from the mines of Treeton, is the pleasant farming village of Ulley, where Rotherham and Sheffield businessmen eat hearty lunches in the 'away from it all' setting of the Royal Oak, a former farmhouse, in part over 400 years old, and sail in their yachts on the reservoir at the foot of the steep hill west of the village. Between the red-brick mining villages of Dinnington and Thurcroft are the partly Norman church of Throapham St John and the attractive limestone village of Laughton-en-le-Morthen. Morthen, whose name refers to a gathering of 'moor men', was, like neighbouring Hallamshire, a sub-division of the local wapentake. At Laughton are the tree-embowered motte of a Norman castle, a village school still housed in a building of the year of the Gunpowder Plot, and a majestic church with the most beautiful spire in the Riding. Crocketted, and with a double set of flying buttresses joining it to its tower, it reaches a height of 185 feet, and soaring high above the trees gives the surrounding flat countryside something of the look of 'Constable country'. Tower and spire and much of the body of the church are fifteenth-century, but there is an Anglo-Saxon north doorway and there are round Norman pillars on the north side of the nave.

Yes, South Yorkshire is full of surprises and, neglected by most writers of topography, who seem to think that practically all that is worth seeing in the West Riding is in the Dales, really deserves a book to itself. The county council, which, in an effort to make local people conscious of belonging to a county worth belonging to, publishes its own newspaper and sells South Yorkshire blazer badges and ties, is in the course of bringing out a series of leaflets on villages, churches, castles and follies. One of the most interesting places in the county is Wentworth

Woodhouse, now the Lady Mabel College of Physical Education but once one of the biggest stately homes in England. It is really two houses in one. They stand back to back; one faces west, the other east, but there is a considerable difference in level between the two, and there is no direct communication around the building as there is in most large houses. Strange to say, they were both built for the same man, Thomas Wentworth, marquis of Rockingham, and the second was started before the first was completed and has a front 600 feet long. As if all this were not folly enough, the grounds are full of follies. One of them stands almost in the back gardens of some suburban houses just to the north of Rotherham, not far from Kirkstead Abbey Grange. This is Keppel's column, 115 feet high and commemorating the acquittal of the second lord Rockingham's friend, Admiral Viscount Keppel, who had been accused of incompetence at the battle of Ushant in 1778 when the enemy (French) ships escaped. Rockingham, a former Whig prime minister, thought that Keppel was merely being used as a scapegoat for the Tory politicians who had embezzled funds which should have been used to keep the fleet in repair so that it could achieve success in battle. Another of the Wentworth Woodhouse follies, Hoober Stand, is a hill-top pyramid which can be seen from afar, high above the pit-head gear and slag heaps which are themselves so prominent in the landscape (though in fairness to the relevant authorities it should be added that many of the slag heaps are either being wiped away or grassed-over and planted with trees). The Stand was built in honour of George II and to commemorate the suppression of the Jacobite rebellion in 1746 and the peace treaty of Aix-la-Chapelle in 1748. By climbing 155 spiral steps inside it, one can reach a balcony from which it is said one can see the towers and spires of 50 churches in Yorkshire and Derbyshire.

Wentworth itself has two churches, one with a spire and one with a tower. The spired one, which is another landmark visible from afar, is a large building and is probably the best example in the Riding of the work of J. L. Pearson, although it does seem a little out of place in rural Yorkshire. It was paid for by the Fitzwilliams, who succeeded the Wentworths at the big house, and it replaced the towered church, which is now a ruin and where all that remains intact is the Wentworth family chapel, and even this bears notices to warn visitors of danger from falling stones. It was long thought that the chapel was the burial place of Thomas Wentworth, earl of Strafford, whose memorial is there, but there is a possibility that his remains lie elsewhere. Strafford was the minister of Charles I who was betrayed by his master and beheaded by Parliament in 1641 on a number of charges including one of planning to use an Irish army against England. His ghost is said to haunt the west block of Wentworth Woodhouse, which incorporates some doorways and windows from a house he built in 1630. After the earl's death, his widow retired to the village of Hooton Roberts, and when she died in 1688 was buried in the chancel of the church there. In 1895 some workmen discovered three skeletons in that chancel – one with its vertebrae severed as though it had been beheaded! Was this the skeleton of Strafford? Many people think so, although the idea has been disputed by a number of competent historians.

Hooton Roberts church is on a bank above the traffic of the main road from Rotherham to Doncaster. On the other side of that busy road is a marvellous old barn, sweet with the scent of hay, said to have been a tithe barn. It is another of South Yorkshire's many surprises. Yet another is the little church of Ravenfield, a real estate church, well away from any village but adjacent to the grounds of a big house. It was designed by John Carr in a very primitive Gothic style, at a time, in the middle of the eighteenth century, when most architects, Carr included, were building classical churches, and the Gothick style, as it was called, was something of a folly in itself. The church is up a tree-shaded lane off the Hooton Roberts–Bramley road, and is worth seeking out if only for its pleasant situation – miniature sewage works notwithstanding.

Another green spot is Wath-on-Dearne churchyard. Wath is a mining town, but the area around the church is pleasant enough. The church itself has a Norman tower and Norman pillars in a nave lit from two fine brass chandeliers, while in a corner is a bell made in the year of the Spanish Armada but not rung since 1935. Many of the district's churches have objects of unusual interest. The font of about 1500 at Aston must be unique, incorporating as it does what is possibly a self-portrait of the mason who made it.

Perhaps the most pleasant and surprising of all the Rotherham district's surprises lies close to the dusty colliery town of Maltby – a sheltered little green valley, with limestone cliffs and woodland, which is carpeted with daffodils in Spring, and, in the middle of all its beauty, the tall grey walls of the transepts of Roche Abbey, a Cistercian house founded in 1247. The lead from the abbey's roofs was removed at the Dissolution by lighting fires beneath them, and little else remains apart from the gatehouse. Close to it is the small, early nineteenth-century house where the Department of the Environment's custodian lives. How lucky people like him are to be able to live in such delightful spots, and how lucky he is in particular to be able to look out of his window on to this delectable landscape 'improved' by Capability Brown as part of his plan for the grounds of nearby Sandbeck Hall, the home of the earl of Scarbrough. Contrary to many people's ideas about South Yorkshire, there is still a considerable degree of truth in the opening paragraph of *Ivanhoe,* a book set in

that pleasant district of Merry England which is watered by the Don . . . the beautiful hills and valleys which lie between Sheffield and the pleasant town of Doncaster.

CHAPTER TWELVE

Doncaster

The Doncaster district is a big one. In the west of the district we are back on the magnesium limestone belt, and in the east in the marshlands of the Humber estuary. There is an amazing difference in scene as one passes from the brick-built mining towns on the fringes of Barnsley and Rotherham into the limestone area, and nowhere is it more marked than where the A.635 abruptly forsakes the grimy ribbon development of Goldthorpe for the delightful countryside around the delectable village of Hickleton. On the village green, near a crucifix erected to the memory of Edward VII, is a notice informing the traveller that the earl of Halifax invites him to rest awhile and enjoy Hickleton, and it is a place to be savoured. Lord Halifax is the lord of the manor, but his Georgian family house is now a Sue Ryder Home. His family have endowed the parish church with pictures and plate and carvings, making it into something of a museum and yet an obviously well-loved place of worship. The old south porch of the largely Perpendicular building has been detached and re-erected as a lych-gate, and a surprising one at that. Grinning at us through glass in one wall are three skulls, a startling reminder of our own mortality.

The earls of Halifax are patrons of another church at Hooton Pagnell – a complete Norman church of west tower and nave and a chancel lengthened in the thirteenth century, set in another lovely stone village, whose hall has a fourteenth-century gatehouse. There is more Norman work in the churches at Marr, just beyond Hickleton on the same busy main road, and at Brodsworth a mile or two to the north, but

193

here one is reminded that despite the beauty of the countryside one is still in a mining area: the church has had to be supported by scaffolding because of the threat of subsidence.

Doncaster is the headquarters of the northern division of the National Coal Board, and as in the Barnsley and Rotherham areas, beauty and ugliness, coalmines and farming communities rub shoulders with one another. Fishlake, for example, close to the mining village of Stainforth, is an attractive little place on the north bank of the Don with rose-decked cottages and a church hidden by trees – one of the most prosperous looking and impressive of all the West Riding's churches, whose south porch shelters one of the finest Norman doorways in England. Fishlake is in the marshlands, where there are two old towns, still pleasant although the newer development is bigger in area than their ancient core. One is Thorne, by Thorne Waste, brick-built and partly Georgian; the other is Hatfield on the edge of Hatfield Chase and not far from the South Humberside marshes of the Isle of Axholme. It is a place with a grand church, light and airy with a massive central tower and what is a welcome boon to 'church crawlers' used to parking their cars on dangerous bends in country lanes and hunting town centres for a de-restricted area – a large car park. Hatfield is probably Bede's Heathfield, the place where in 633 Edwin, the first Christian king of Northumbria was killed in battle by the pagan Penda of Mercia. And it has other royal connections. The manor house, with a twelfth-century window and other features from the sixteenth, seventeenth and eighteenth centuries, was the birthplace of William of Hatfield, son of Edward III, and was given by King Charles II, along with the Chase, to Cornelius Vermuyden, the fen drainer. Although his work in draining the Chase produced what is now a rich 14,000-acre belt of corn-growing arable land, he met with a lot of opposition. His mistake in altering the course of the Don did not help, but besides that the Chase teemed with red deer and its sluggish rivers with salmon, so the foresters, anxious for their livelihood, did what they could to keep things as they were. They attacked the Dutch workmen, who had set about their great task armed only with their native water-engineering genius, picks, shovels and hundreds of small primitive windpumps, and drowned them in their own dykes. In the end, however, Vermuyden and his workforce of 3,000, some of them Protestant refugees from persecution in the Low Countries, triumphed. They settled at Sandtoft in what was then Lincolnshire, but they were not welcome and in 1686 the local people burnt down their chapel and they moved to the Thorne and Hatfield area. There they were joined by other religious refugees – Huguenots from France. Vermuyden is still remembered in the names of inns and streets as he is in the Goole area, and Dutch names occur in the telephone book in a district where the older houses are roofed with Dutch tiles.

Much of the produce of the rich agricultural land Vermuyden helped to create is sold in the market at Doncaster. Hundreds of stalls surround the Market Hall, built in 1870 as the Corn Exchange, and create an atmosphere somehow not only less claustrophobic but really refreshing when compared with that of the town's new Arndale Centre. The original parish church of the town, St Mary Magdalene's, apparently stood on the site of the market; the present one, St George's is one of the most magnificent buildings in the county. If Rotherham church is the finest medieval church in South Yorkshire, Doncaster church must surely be the finest nineteenth-century one. A splendid cruciform building with a soaring central tower; unless one was told one would probably not recognize it as nineteenth-century at all. It has some affinity with our great cathedrals – not surprisingly perhaps, since it is the work of Sir Gilbert Scott, to whom we owe the present external appearance of the 'medieval' cathedrals at Ripon, Worcester, Lichfield and Chester. The peal of bells and the pulpit were, however, the creation of Lord Grimthorpe, who was a constant thorn in Scott's flesh. Newly cleaned, St George's stands amongst the wastelands once covered by medieval Doncaster. It was here that Thomas of Lancaster assembled his forces for the rising that was to lead to his execution, and it was here in 1536 that the rebels of the Pilgrimage of Grace surrendered to the agents of King Henry VIII.

St George's is not the only church in the town designed by Sir Gilbert Scott; another is St James', in the creation of which he again had some help, or rather interference, from Lord Grimthorpe, who altered the spire at his own expense. It was built by the shareholders of the Great Northern Railway Company, whose chairman was Grimthorpe's father, for Doncaster has long been a locomotive building centre – the birthplace of the *Flying Scotsman* and of the record breaking *Mallard*. British Rail's double arrow sign features in the district's coat-of-arms.

Another industry for which Doncaster is well known is sweet making. It is the home of Parkinson's Royal Doncaster Butterscotch, which, its wrapper tells us, is,

> *As supplied by permission (and to no other party was the same granted) to the Queen and Royal Family on their visit to Doncaster in 1851 . . . And extensively patronized by the Nobility, Clergy and Gentry.*

It got its name because it is made from *scorched* butter and sugar.

Parkinson's butterscotch finds a ready market on Doncaster Common on race days, for Doncaster is the home of the St Leger, the famous race for three-year-olds which was first run in 1776 and named after its originator, Colonel Anthony St Leger. Racing has been a feature of life in the town since at least 1703 and the gentry used to stay in the once elegant Georgian and Regency houses in the terraces in South Parade at the southern end of town near the racecourse itself, which still has some attractive nineteenth-century cast-iron grandstands. The houses are still impressive, but their stucco is peeling and their restoration looks like another job for the Civic Trust. Today if racegoers stay overnight in Doncaster at all they use one of the big hotels like the Danum whose name is that of a Roman station which once stood here on the road between Lincoln and York. Doncaster itself means 'the camp by the Don'. Another of the town's leading hotels is Punch's which is said to be shaped like Mr Punch's head, although it takes a lot of imagination to see it.

Apart from the parish church, perhaps the most imposing

building in the town is James Paine's Mansion House, built as a home for the mayor during his year of office, and one of only three in England, the others being at London and York. It was built in 1750. Paine also added two wings, to house library and chapel, to Cusworth Hall, in the country just to the north of town, for William Wrightson, the ex-M.P. son of a rich lawyer from Hemsworth. A really beautiful stone house by Platt of Rotherham with five bays and a central pediment over the Venetian window of its north front, its crumbling walls are being refaced and it has been converted into a museum of South Yorkshire industry.

Close to the hall but on the other side of the A.1(M) is the motte or artificial mound on which the keep of a Norman castle once stood. The keep was probably timber-built and nothing remains of it, but a few miles away at Conisbrough is one of the finest castles in Yorkshire, its white limestone keep, high above the chimney pots of a small mining town, amazingly intact. The reason for its fine state of preservation is that by the time of the Civil War the castle had already been abandoned and was incapable of putting up any great resistance to attackers because gate, bridge and curtain wall had fallen down. It was not used therefore to resist the Parliamentary forces and they saw no reason to slight it as they did the other West Riding fortresses. The keep is an unusual shape – a cylindrical tower with a splayed base clasped by six wedge-shaped buttresses which rise as turrets above the level of the keep proper. Walter Scott, who wrote *Ivanhoe* while staying at nearby Sprotborough, described Conisbrough in that book as Coningsburgh, the ancient Saxon fortress of Athelstane the thane. In fact the keep was newly built at the time of which Scott was writing – the reign of Richard I. Its builder was Hamelin Plantagenet, half-brother of Richard's father, Henry II. The original earthworks, however, had been laid out by William de Warrenne, earl of Surrey, to whom the land had been given by the Conqueror. But even before that there had been a fort at Conisbrough – the name means 'king's fortress' – probably on the opposite hill where the church stands, and at the time of the Conquest the manor was held by King Harold.

There are remains of another castle at Tickhill, but here the keep, which *was* held against Parliament, was demolished down to its foundations, and the most impressive remains are the gatehouse and curtain wall. One of only two castles to hold out for John on Richard I's return from captivity – the other was Nottingham – it was also one of only five places in England where royal jousting tournaments were held. It is not the castle, whose domestic quarters are still lived in, that is the attraction of Tickhill for today's visitor however, but the fine church, a large Perpendicular building begun about 1340 with an unforgettable tower, 124 feet high. Its interior is perfect apart from a flimsy, new, spire-shaped canopy over the font which looks like part of a modern set for a Shakespeare play performed with the minimum of scenery. Perhaps in an age with better taste than our own it will be removed, for it merely cheapens an otherwise superb building. Tickhill's is the church of a pleasant little town which has an attractive market cross at the road junction at its centre. Dating from 1777, it is an open rotunda on eight columns, rather like the famous cross at Beverley in Humberside.

Another attractive little town is Bawtry, a few miles to the east, once an important port on the River Idle, a tributary of the Trent, and an important staging post for travellers on the Great North Road. Its broad main street is also the Market Square, and here is the Crown Hotel, an old coaching house, which, according to tradition, was once the haunt of Dick Turpin. Just down the street is a pleasant little court of fashionable shops and cafés which is crowded with visitors at the height of the summer tourist season. Bawtry always was the traditional gateway to Yorkshire from the South. Here the High Sheriff welcomed royal visitors to the county, and here, in 1541, Sir Robert Bowes met Henry VIII. Sir Robert had with him 200 gentlemen dressed in velvet and 4,000 tall yeomen and serving men on horseback, and in the name of the shire, which had not long before been in Henry's bad books because of its links with the Pilgrimage of Grace, presented the king with a purse containing £900 in gold. Bawtry, the gateway town, is perhaps an appropriate place for us to leave the county of which the seventeenth-century historian Fuller (who is unlikely to have been a Lancashireman!) wrote:

One may call and justify this to be the best shire in England.

INDEX

The numerals in bold type refer to the figure numbers of the illustrations

Abbeydale, 181
Acomb Moor, 55
Adel, **2**, 132, 133, 145
Adlingfleet, 48
Ainley Top, 106, 109
Aire, River, 12, 37, 45, 47, 134, 153
Aire and Calder Navigation, 37, 46
Airedale, 129
 Heifer, 130
Airmyn, 45
Aislabie family, 51
Akroyd, Edward, 117–18
Akroydon, 118
Aldborough, 26, 49, 93
Almondbury, 12, 94, 95, 100, 103, 172
Alphin Pike, 82
Alverthorpe, 13
Alwoodley, 140, 143
Apperley Bridge, 128
Appletreewick, 65
Architects
 Adam, Robert, 55, 137, 162
 Baker, Sir Herbert, 137
 Barry, Sir Charles, 117, 137
 Bodley, G. F., 172
 Brodrick, Cuthbert, 149
 Butterfield, William, 44, 45
 Carr, John, 115, 137, 163, 177, 185, 191
 Chantrell, Dennis, 100–1, 132, 145–6,
  147, 155–6
 Comper, Sir Ninian, 158
 Dayston family, 172
 Grimthorpe, Lord, 147, 195–6
 Hardwick, Philip, 151
 Kaye, Joseph, 95–6
 Lockwood and Mawson, 125, 126, 149,
  151
 Mallinson and Healey, 127
 Moore, Temple, 44, 60, 177
 Paine, James, 45, 162, 163, 197
 Paxton, Sir Joseph, 119
 Pearson, F. L., 158
 Pearson, J. L., 147, 158, 190
 Platt family of Rotherham, 197
 Poulson, John, 131
 Pritchett, J. P., 97
 Rickman, Thomas, 147, 168, 170
 Scott, Sir George Gilbert, 50, 99, 101,
  117, 140, 147, 151, 158, 187, 195, 196
 Tapper, Sir Walter, 60

Waterhouse, Alfred, 125, 150, 151
Wheeler, Sir Charles, 137
Womersley, J. L., 183
Wood, Edgar, 97
Ardsley, 167
Armitage Bridge, 96–7, 101
Armley, 131, 139, 169
Armstrong, Thomas, 96
Arncliffe, 67, 68
Arten Gill, 77
arts, the, 20, 39, 91, 98, 122, 126
Aske, Robert, 42
Askern, 27
Asquith, Herbert Henry, 96
Aston, **11**, 192
Attercliffe, 181
Audus, James, 38
Austwick, 15

Badsworth, 22
Barden Tower, 65
Bardsey, 26, 132
Barkisland, 111
Barnoldswick, 14, 80–1
Barnsley, 13, 19–20, 166, 168–71
Barwick-in-Elmet, 13
Batley, 104
Bawtry, 198–9
Beamsley, 65
Beaumont family, 26, 44, 103
Beaumont, Geoffrey, 100
Beaumont Park, 23
Bentley, Phyllis, 92
Bessemer, Henry, 182
Biggerside, 75
Bingley, 27
 Lord, 138
Birstall, 105
Bishopthorpe, **17**, 30, 41
Bolling Hall, 127
Bolton Abbey, **9**, 65
Bolton-by-Bowland, 79–80
Bolton Percy, 41
Boothferry, 45
Boroughbridge, **27**, 49, 156
Boston Spa, 27
Boulsover, Thomas, 180
Bowland, 77–80
Bradford, **13**, 14, 26, 27, 121–7, 149
Bradley Woods, 106

Bramham, 132
Park, **18**, 138
Bramhope, 149
Brayton, 32
Brearley, Harry, 180
Bretton, 13, 26
Brigantes, the, 12, 49, 94
Brigflatts, 77
Brighouse, 15, 20, 21, 106, 118
Brimham Rocks, **7**, 62
Brodsworth, 193–4
Brontë family, 64, 92, 105, 112, 128–9
Brook family, 101–2
Brooke family, 96, 101
Brotherton, 30
Browsholme, 14, 79
Buckden, 66
Moor, 24
Buckstones, 22
Burmantofts, 134, 150
Burnsall, 65–6

Calder, River, 12, 37, 100, 109
Calderdale, 16, 24, **26**, 109
canals, 21, 27, 37–8, 46, 86, 109–10
Cannon Hall, 171
Caractacus, 49
Carlton-in-Balne, 44
Cartwright, Edmund, 123
Castleford, 153
Castleshaw, 26
Cawood, 30–1, 42, 56, 178
Cawthorne, 171–2
Chapel-le-Dale, 70
Charles I, 26, 55
Chevin, The, 12
Chew Valley, 82
Chippendale, Thomas, 138, 162
Civil War, 42, 55, 64, 104, 136, 148–9, 155,
177, 197, 198
Clapham, 69
Cleckheaton, 104
Cliffe Castle, 129–30
Clifford family, 42, 64–5, 158
Colne, River, 12, 21, 91, 94
Colne Bridge, 94
Colne valley, 91
Community of the Resurrection, 99–100
Conisbrough, 26, 197
Conistone, 67
Cooper Bridge, 91, 110
Copley, 118
Cowgill, 77
beck, 74
Cowick, 44–5

Cragg Vale, 112–3
Craven, Sir William, 65
Craven Heifer, 130
Cray, **1**
Crofton, 161
Cromwell, Oliver, 43, 55
Cromwell Lake, 21
Crosland Moor, 93
Crossley family, 118–9
Cross Wood, 25
customs, 15–16, 21, 98, 100, 101
Cusworth, 197

Dacre, 63
Dacre family, 42
Dalton, 13
Darcy family, 41, 42, 135
Darnley, Henry Stuart, Lord, 135
Darton, 172, 173
Dawnay family, 44–5
Dearne, River, 174
Dee, River, 76
Deerstones, 22
De Lacy family, 26, 81, 82–3, 91, 134, 153,
154
Delius, Frederick, 122
Delph, 81, 83, 87
Denaby Ings, 24
Denby Dale, 13, 104
Denshaw, 81, 82, 83
Dent Town, **24**, 75, 76–7
Devil's Arrows, 49
De Warrenne, William, 26, 197
Dewsbury, 13, 99, 100
dialect, 13–14
Diggle, 81
brook, 85
Dinnington, 189
Dobcross, 81, 82, 83, 85, 86, 87–8
Doestones, 22
Don, River, 12, 47, 180, 183
Doncaster, 24, 192, 194, 195–7
Drax, 390
dry-stone walls, 67–8
Duckworth, Francis, 80
Duke of Wellington's Regiment, 115
Dutch River, 47

Earby, 81
Eastoft, 47
East Riddlesden, 130
Ecclesfield, 172
Eccleshill, 139
Edgerton, 96–7
Edward I, 30

Index

Edward II, 26, 30, 41, 156
Edward IV, 41, 161
Edward VII, 136
Elland, 24, 111, 114, 120
Elsecar, 167–8
Emley, 24, 91, 104
Engels, Friedrich, 95

Fairburn Ings, 23
Fairfax family, 26, 42–3, 55, 136
Fawkes, Guy, 16
Firth, Mark, 182
Fishlake, 47, 194
Fixby Hall, 93
food and drink, 16, 19, 29–30, 101, 109, 168, 171, 182, 196
Forster, W. E., 126
Foster Beck, 62, 63
Fountains Abbey, **6**, 26, 52, 106
  Hall, 26, 52
Fox, George, 77
Frere, W. H., 100
Friezeland, 84
Fringill, 62
Frith, William Powell, 59–60
Fulneck, 127

Gaping Ghyl, 69
Garsdale, 74, 75, 76
Gisburn, 21, 78, 80
Golcar, 14
Goldthorpe, 193
Gomersal, 105
Goole, 12, 27, 38, 45–7
Gordale Scar, 69
Gore, Charles, 100
Grange, 83, 84
Grassington, 25, 66
Great Mitton, **12**, 79
Great Whernside, 66
Greenfield, 16, 82
Greenhow Hill, 63
Greetland, 111
Greta, River, 69
Grimethorpe, 20
Guiseley, 16, 128

Halifax, **14**, 19, 20, 25, 27, 70, 106, 110, 111, 112, 113–20
  Building Society, 117, 118
Hallamshire, 189
Hallé, Sir Charles, 122
Hardcastle Crags, 120
Harden Moss, 22
Harewood, **19**, 26, 137

Harold, King, 197
Harrogate, 27, 56–61
Hartley, David, 112–3
Hartshead, 128
  Moor, 92
Hatfield, 194
  Chase, 24, 25, 194–5
Haworth, **28**, 128–9
Hazlewood Castle, 30
Headingley, 140, 147–8
Hebble beck, 114
Heath, 162–3
Hebden Bridge, 110, 120
Heck, 44
Heights, 83
Helme, 101–2
Hemsworth, 197
Henry I, 32
Henry III, 30
Henry VI, 79–80, 158
Henry VIII, 198
Hensall, 44
Heptonstall, **10**, 110, 113
Hickleton, 193
Hirst, Joseph, 102
Holbeck, 144, 145
Holme River, 94
  Moss, 103
  Valley, 91, 103
Holmfirth, 103
Honley, 97
Hoober Stand, 190
Hood, Robin, 99, 156–7
Hook, 45
Hooton Pagnell, 193
Hooton Roberts, 191
Horbury, 163
Horsfall, William, 93
Horton-in-Ribblesdale, 70
How, William Walsham, 158
Howard family, dukes of Norfolk, 44, 179, 183, 187–8
Howgill Fells, 75
Howley Hall, 104
Hubberholme, 66
Huddersfield, 14, 15, 20, 21, 24, 27, 91, 93–9, 100, 103, 106, 125
Huddlesey, 38
Huddleston, Trevor, 99
Humber, River, 22, 34, 45, 47
Hunslet, 144, 145
Huntsman, Benjamin, 181

Idle, River, 198

Ilkley, 27, 69, 130
  Moor, 22
immigrants in West Riding, 15, 19, 96, 119, 122–3, 123–4, 127, 140, 143–4, 195
Ingilby family, 55
Ingleborough, 69, 70
  caves, 69
Ingleton, 69
Ingram family, 135–6
Iron and steel industry, 63, 106, 133, 172, 174–5, 179–183, 184, 185

Jews in West Riding, 122–3, 143–4
John, King, 30, 198

Kagan, Joseph, Lord, 111
Keighley, 27, 129–30
Keppel's column, 190
Kettlewell, 66
Kildwick Hall, 130
Kilnsey Crag, 66
Kimberworth, 185
Kingsley, Charles, 68
Kingstone, 169–70
Kippax, 32, 132–3
Kirkburton, 100, 103
Kirk Hammerton, 49
Kirkheaton, 94, 100, 103
Kirklees Priory, 92, 99
Kirkstall, 133, 147
  Abbey, **4**, 26, 81, 133–4, 150
Kirkstead Abbey Grange, 185
Kirkthorpe, 161
Knaresborough, **8**, 26, 55–6
Knights Templar, 40–1, 134–5
knur and spell, 111–2

Lancaster, Thomas, Earl of, 26, 41, 156, 195
Langcliffe, 69
Langstrothdale, 66
Lascelles family, 137
Laughton-en-le-Morthen, 189
Lead, 42
Leathley, 68
Ledsham, 23, 26, 132
Ledston, 132
Leeds, 14, **20**, 20, 21, 23, 24, 131–2, 134, 135, 138–52
Lindley, 97
Linton, 65, 67
Little Horton, 127
Littondale, 67, 68
Lister, Samuel Cunliffe, Lord Masham, 123

Liversedge, 92, 104–5
Locke, Joseph, 169
Lockwood, 23, 100–1, 102, 146
Longley, 95
Long Marston, 55
Longroyd Bridge, 93, 101
Longwood, 21, 102
Lothersdale, 64
Lotherton Hall, 138
Low Laithe, 63
Low Moor, 127
Loxley, River, 180
Luddenden, 112
Luddendenfoot, 111, 112
Luddites, 92–3
Lydgate, 83–4

Malham, 14, 67
  Cove, 68–9
  Tarn, 25, 68
Manningham, **13**, 123–4, 127
Markenfield Hall, 52
Marr, 193
Marsden, 15, 24, 26, 93
Marston Moor, 26, 55
Mary , Queen of Scots, 135, 178–9
Masbrough, 184, 185
Meltham, 26, 102
Meltham Mills, 101
Metcalf, John (Blind Jack of Knaresborough), 59, 106
Methley, 136–7, 147
Middlesmoor, 62
Middleton Railway, 145
Milnsbridge, 93
mining
  coal, 30, 145, 166–7, 182
  iron, 63, 174–5, 194
  lead, 63–4
Mirfield, 99–100, 105
Monck, George, duke of Albermarle, 43
Monk Bretton, 173–4
Monk Fryston, 39–40
monks and monasteries, 26, 32–4, 39, 52, 65, 80, 99–100, 106, 133, 162, 172–3
Montagu, Lady Mary Wortley, 175
Montgomery, James, 127
Moor Monkton, 55
Moore, Henry, 137
Moravians, 127–8
Morley, 27, 147, 149
Murray, Matthew, 145

Netherthong, 100, 101
Netherton, 13

Newby Hall, 55
New Hey Fell, 23
New Tame, 85, 87
Nidd, River, **8**, 56
Nidderdale, 62
Normanton, 161
Nostell Priory, 162–3
Nun Appleton, 43

Oakworth, 129
Oastler, Richard, 93, 127–8, 147
Ossett, 27
Otley, 130,162
Oulton, 147
Ouse, River, 22, 28, 33, 45, 48
Ousefleet, 48
Outlane, 109

Parker family, 43, 79
Pateley Bridge, 62, 63
Paulinus, St, 100
Paythorne, 21
Peak District National Park, 22
Penistone, 22, 172
Pennines, 11, 22, 25
Pennine Way, 22
Pen-y-ghent, 12, 70
Percy family, 41, 45, 52–3
Pilgrimage of Grace, 42, 80, 195, 198
Platt family, 87–8
Pollington, 44
Pontefract, 23, **25**, 26, 81, 153–6, 163
Porter Brook, 180
Pots and Pans, 82
pottery industry, 144, 185–6
Priestley, Joseph, 131

Ramsden family, 94–5, 97, 110
Ranmoor, 182
Rathmell, 14
Rastrick, 20, 116
Ravenfield, 191
Ravensthorpe, 13
Rawcliffe, 45
Ribble, River, 21
Ribblehead, 69, 77
Ribblesdale, 70, 73
Richard II, 156
Rimington, 80
  William of, 80
Ripley, 26, 55
Ripon, **5**, 23, 49–51
Ripponden, 111
Rivelin, River, 180
Roche Abbey, 192

Rockingham, Charles, second Marquess of, 190
Rockingham Pottery, 185–6
Rockley Abbey, 174, 175
Roebucks, 22
Roman Yorkshire, 12, 26, 28–9, 49, 63, 109, 153, 186, 196
Rotherham, 20, 184–9
Rotherham, Thomas, 188
Rothwell, 20, 134
Roundhay, 132, 140
Royston, 172–3
Rudding Park, 93
Ryburn, River, 111

Saddleworth, 82–3
Sadler, Michael, 93
St Leger, The, 196
Salt, Sir Titus, 123
Saltaire, 123
Salterhebble, 109, 110
Sandal Magna, 161
Sandbeck Hall,192
Savile Family, 104, 113, 136
Sawley Abbey, 14, 80
Saxton, 42
Scammonden, 21
Scott, Sir Walter, 197
Scouthead, 84
Sedbergh, 14, 74, 75–6
Selby, **3**, 14, 32–9, 42
Settle, 20, 27, 69
Sheaf, River, 180
Sheffield, 14, 19, **22**, 24, 176–83, 184
Sherburn-in-Elmet, 13, 31–2, 41
Shibden Dale, 112
Shipley, 123
Shipton, Mother, 56
Silkstone, 167, 172, 173
Skell, River, **6**, 51
Skelmanthorpe, 13
Skelton, 55
Skipton, **15**, 26, 64–5
Skirfare, River, 68
Slack, 109
Slaidburn, 79
Slaithwaite, 14, 15, 20, 27, 92, 102
Slingsby family, 55, 57
Smeaton, James, 110
Smelthouses, 63
Smith family of Tadcaster, 29–30
Smithies, 174
Snaith, 45, 47
South Milford, 32, 43–4
Sowerby Bridge, 110, 112

Index

Spen valley, 104
Spofforth, 52
sport and recreation, 12, 20–3, 32, 49, 91, 189, 196
Sprotborough, 197
Standedge, 86, 91
Stapleton family, 44
Starbotton, 66
Steanor Bottom, 109
Steel industry (see Iron and steel)
Steeton Hall, 44
Stocks Reservoir, 78
Stoodley Pike, **26**, 120
Strafford, Thomas Wentworth, Earl of, 191
Strid, The, 47
Studley Royal, 51
Stump Cross Caverns, 62
Swinefleet, 47
Swinton, 186
Sykehouse, 47
Sykes, Susan (Mrs. Sunderland), 20

Tadcaster, 28–30, 32
Talbot family, earls of Shrewsbury, 174, 178
Tame, River, 81, 85, 87
Tame Bridge, 85
Tankersley, 174
Templeborough, 186
Temple Hirst, 40–1, 42
Temple Newsam, **16**, 134–6, 144
textile industry, 39, 52, 62–3, 64, 77, 84–9, 91–4, 104, 105, 106, 110, 114, 116, 118, 121–2, 123, 138, 139, 140–1, 144–5, 157, 172–3
Thorne, 24, 25, 194
Thorner, 25, 134
Thornhill, 104
Thornhill family, 93, 96, 104
Thorpe Common, 185
Thornton, 128
Thornton Forge, 69
Throapham St John, 189
Tickhill, **23**, 26, 198
Tinsley viaduct, 184
Tockwith, 55
Todmorden, 109
Tong, 127
Towton, 41–2, 161
Trent, River, 48, 198
Trollope, Anthony, 188
Trough of Bowland, 78–9
Trow Gill, 69
Turpin, Dick, 198
Twiss valley, 69

Ulley, 189
Upper Haugh, 186
Uppermill, 82, 86, 88
Ure, River, 12, 61

vegetation, 25, 70, 78
Vermuyden, Cornelius, 46–7, 194–5

Waddington, 80
Wadsworth, 109
Wakefield, 19, **21,** 23, 42, 109, 123, 153, 156–61
Wales, 13
Walton, 13, 132
Walton Hall Park, 23
Wars of the Roses, 26, 41–2, 55, 79–80, 158, 161
Washburndale, 62
Waterton, Charles, 23
Wath (Nidderdale), 62
Wath-on-Dearne, 191–2
Went, River, 12
Wentworth, 189–91
Wentworth Castle, 175
Wentworth family, 26, 190–1
Wentworth Woodhouse, 189–91
Wesley, John, 110, 182
    Samuel Sebastian, 146
Wetherby, 23
Wharfe, River, **9**, 12, 65, 130
Wharfedale, **1**, 22, 65–8
Whernside, 70
Whiston, 189
Whitewell, 23
Whitgift, 47
Whitkirk, 134
Whitley Beaumont, 103–4
Wilberlee, 22
wild life, 23–5, 70, 78
William I, 26, 32
Wilshaw, 102
Wilson, Sir Harold, 111, 124
Wincobank, 180
Wistow, 42
Wolfstones, 22
Wolsely, Cardinal Thomas, 30–1, 56, 178
Wood family, earls of Halifax, 136, 193
Woodhouse Moor, 134
Woodsome Hall, 26, 92
Wooldale, 22
Woolley, 14
Woolroad, 86
Wortley, 175
Worth Valley, 128–9
    Railway, 129

Index

Wragby, 161–2
Wyke, 127

Yockenthwaite, 13, 26

York, 11, 12, 28, 30
  Richard, duke of, 158, 161
Yorkshire Dales National Park, 22, 74
Yorkshire Post, 12